Women Explorers

Annie Montague Alexander
Alexander
Naturalist and Fossil Hunter

Women Explorers

Women Explorers

Annie Montague Alexander
Naturalist and Fossil Hunter

Louise Chipley Slavicek

Introduction: Milbry Polk,
author of *Women of Discovery*

CHELSEA HOUSE
PUBLISHERS
A Haights Cross Communications Company

Philadelphia

CHELSEA HOUSE PUBLISHERS
VP, NEW PRODUCT DEVELOPMENT Sally Cheney
DIRECTOR OF PRODUCTION Kim Shinners
CREATIVE MANAGER Takeshi Takahashi
MANUFACTURING MANAGER Diann Grasse

Staff for ANNIE MONTAGUE ALEXANDER
ASSOCIATE EDITOR Kate Sullivan
PRODUCTION EDITOR Megan Emery
PHOTO EDITOR Sarah Bloom
SERIES & COVER DESIGNER Terry Mallon
LAYOUT 21st Century Publishing and Communications, Inc.

A Haights Cross Communications ✦ Company

http://www.chelseahouse.com

First Printing

9 8 7 6 5 4 3 2 1

Library of Congress Cataloging-in-Publication Data

Slavicek, Louise Chipley, 1956–
   Annie Montague Alexander : naturalist and fossil hunter/by Louise
   Chipley Slavicek.
      p. cm.—(Women explorers)
Includes bibliographical references and index.
   ISBN 0-7910-7710-1
   1. Alexander, Annie Montague, 1867–1950—Juvenile literature.
2. Zoologists—United States—Biography—Juvenile literature.
[1. Alexander, Annie Montague, 1867–1950. 2. Naturalists.
3. Women—Biography.] I. Title. II. Series.
QL31.A555S62 2004
590'.92—dc22
                                                        2003026248

Table of Contents

Introduction

By Milbry Polk

Curiosity is one of the most compelling forces of human life. Our desire to understand who and what and where we are drives us restlessly to explore and to comprehend what we see. Every historical era is known by the individuals who sought to expand our boundaries of time and space and knowledge. People such as Alexander the Great, Ibn Battuta, Marco Polo, Ferdinand Magellan, Hernando de Soto, Meriwether Lewis, William Clark, Charles Darwin, Sir Richard Burton, Roald Amundsen, Jacques Cousteau, Edmund Hillary, Tenzing Norgay, Thor Hyerdahl, and Neil Armstrong are men whose discoveries changed our worldview. They were explorers, leaders into the unknown. This series is about a handful of individuals who have been left out of the history books but whose feats loom large, whose discoveries changed the way we look at the world. They are women explorers.

WHAT MAKES SOMEONE AN EXPLORER?

The desire to know what lies beyond the next hill—the desire to explore—is one of the most powerful of human impulses. This drive makes us unique among the species with which we share our earth. Curiosity helped to impel our remote ancestors out of Africa. It is what spread them in waves throughout the world where they settled; curiosity helped them adapt to the many environments they encountered.

Myths of all cultures include the memories of early explorations. These myths were the means by which people explained to themselves and taught their children about life, about the world around them, and about death. Myths helped people make sense of the inexplicable forces of nature and the strangeness of new lands and peoples. The few myths and legends that have come down to us are the stories of early exploration.

What makes someone an explorer? The qualities required are not unique. We are born explorers. Every child, even in the crib, is reaching out, trying to understand, to take the measure of its own body, then its immediate surroundings, and we continue as we go through life to grasp ever-widening circles of experience and reality. As we grow up, we often lose the excitement of the child, the characteristic that supposedly gave Albert Einstein his ability to see the universe in a new way. What typifies the explorer is not losing this wonderful childlike curiosity. He or she still reaches out. Explorers are open minded—able to look at and accept what they see, rather than to fall back upon preconceived notions. Explorers are courageous, not just in facing physical danger, but also in having the courage to confront failure, ridicule, and laughter, and yet to keep on going. Above all, explorers have the ability to communicate. All insights, observations, and discoveries mean nothing to the wider community if they are not documented and shared. An explorer goes out into the world at some personal risk and discovers something of value and then shares that knowledge with his or her community. Explorers are leaders who look at the world in new ways and in doing so make breakthroughs that enrich all of our lives.

WOMEN EXPLORERS

Women, like men, have always been explorers. Typically in a "hunter-gatherer" society the men hunted animals while the women ventured far from the camps in search of other foods. Though their tasks were different, both were explorers. And, since such societies were almost constantly on the move, women were there for each voyage of discovery. But over time, as cultural groups became more settled, ideas began to change about the role of women in society. Women came to be restricted to the house, the shared courtyard, or the village and began to wear clothing that set them apart. By the time of the Middle Ages often the only way women in the Western world could travel was by going on pilgrimage. The trek to visit holy sites offered women one of the few opportunities to see new places, hear new languages, and meet different people. In fact, the first autobiography in the English language was written by a pilgrim, Margery Kempe (1373–1440), about her journeys throughout Europe and to the Holy Land.

Over time, women became formally excluded from exploration. Of course, some women did manage to find a way around the obstacles. Those who did venture forth went alone or in disguise and often needed men to help them. But their stories were not recorded in official histories; to find their stories one has to dig deep.

About three hundred years ago, the western worldview changed. Beginning in the 1700s, the scientific revolution began to change life for everyone in Europe. Men as well as women were swept up in the excitement to classify and understand every aspect of life on earth. Legions of people went to every corner of the world to see and record what was there. The spirit of adventure began to find new means of expression. New modes of transportation made movement around the world easier and new technologies made recording events and communication less expensive and more vivid.

The findings of these explorers were fascinating to the people back home. Wealthy individuals collected many of the strange insects, botanical specimens, native art, rocks, and other findings, brought back by the explorers into personal collections called Cabinets of Curiosities. These Cabinets of

Curiosities are the forerunners of our modern museums. The desire to collect the unusual financed expeditions, which in turn fostered public interest in exploration. The creation and spread of scientific and popular magazines with stories about expeditions and discoveries enabled the public to learn about the world. By the 1800s, explorers had the status of popular heroes in the public eye. The lure of the unknown gripped society.

Unlike men, women did not have support of institutions such as universities, museums, scientific societies, governments, and the military that sponsored and financed exploration. Until well into the twentieth century, many of these institutions barred women from participation, membership, and especially leadership. Women were thought capable of gathering things such as flowers or rocks for subjects to paint and draw, but men were the ones who studied them, named them, and published books about them. Most women, if they had any specialized education at all, gained it through private tutors. Men went to the university. Men formed and joined scientific societies and the exploring clubs. Men ran the governments, the military, and the press, and archived the collections. Universities and other cultural institutions were open only to the membership of men. Women were generally excluded from them. When these institutions sponsored exploration, they sponsored men. Women not only had to overcome mountains in the wild but also institutions at home.

In the 1800s women were not usually trained or taught academics. Instead, they learned sewing, music, and how to behave as a lady. A woman who managed to learn to write overcame great obstacles. Few managed to do it, but the same spirit that made women into explorers animated their minds in other ways. A few women learned to record what they were doing sufficiently well that at least some of their works have become classics of description and adventure.

Because of them, we know the little we do know about their lives and actions. As the nineteenth century progressed, more and more women were going out collecting, recording, and writing about faraway places. By the late 1800s more women were educated and those who traveled often wrote accounts of their journeys. So, now, in the twenty-first century, we are just beginning to learn about the unknown side of exploration—the women's story—from the accounts that lay buried in our archives.

And what a story it is. For example, one of the first modern women explorers was Maria Sybila Merian, who sailed to Surinam in 1699 at the age of 52. Not content to view the strange flora and fauna that were arriving back in Europe to fill the Cabinets of Curiosity, she wanted to collect and paint insects and animals in their native habitat.

Western women also faced societal obstacles; they generally could not go anywhere without a chaperon. So for a would-be woman explorer, a night in the wild spent in the company of a man who was not a close relative or her husband was unthinkable. And then there were the unsuitable clothes. In many parts of the early modern world it was punishable by death (as it was in Spain in the 1600s) or imprisonment (as it was in America well into the late 1800s) for women to appear in public wearing pants.

The heavy, layered dresses and tight corsets thought necessary for women made traveling very cumbersome. For example, when the Alps began to be climbed by explorers in the 1800s, a few women were caught up in the mania. The first two women to summit the Matterhorn climbed in skirts and corsets. The third woman, an American professor of Latin, Annie Smith Peck (1850–1935), realized the absurdity of leaping crevasses, climbing ice walls, and enduring the winds in a skirt. So, she wore pants. This created such a sensation in 1895 that the Singer Sewing

Machine Company photographed her and included a card with her in climbing gear with every machine it sold.

THE WOMEN EXPLORERS SERIES

When asked why he wanted to climb Mount Everest, George Mallory famously replied, "Because it's there." Perhaps another explorer would answer the same question, "Because I don't know what is there and I want to find out."

Although we all have curiosity, what separates explorers is their willingness to take their curiosity further. Despite the odds, a lack of money, and every imaginable difficulty, they still find a way to go. They do so because they are passionate about life and their passion carries them over the barriers. As you will discover, the women profiled in this series shared that passion. Their passion gave them the strength to face what would seem to be insurmountable odds to most of us. To read their stories is more than learning about the adventure, it is a guide to discovering our own passions. The women in this series, Mary Kingsley, Gertrude Bell, Alexandra David-Néel, Annie Montague Alexander, Sue Hendrickson, and Sylvia Earle, all join the pantheon of explorers, the heroes of our age.

These six women have been chosen because their interests range from geographical to cultural exploration; from traversing the highest mountains to diving to the depths of the oceans; from learning about life far back in time to looking forward into the future. These women are extraordinary leaders and thinkers. They are all individuals who have braved the unknown and challenged the traditional women's roles. Their discoveries have had remarkable and profound effects on what we know about the world. To be an explorer one does not have to be wealthy or have multiple degrees. To be an explorer one must have the desire from within and focus on the destination: the unknown.

Mary Kingsley (1862–1900) was the daughter of an English Victorian gentleman-explorer who believed women did not need to be educated. Mary was kept at home and only tutored in German to translate articles her father wanted to read. But while he was away, she went into his library and educated herself by reading his books. She never married and followed the custom of her day for unmarried women by staying home with her parents. When her parents died she found herself alone—and suddenly free. She purchased a ticket to the Canary Islands with her inheritance. Once there, she learned about the Congo, then considered by the Europeans to be a terrifying place. When Kingsley decided to go to the Congo, she was warned that all she would find would be festering swamplands laced with deadly diseases and cannibals. Kingsley viewed that warning as a challenge. Having used up all her money on the ticket, she outfitted herself as a trader. She returned to the Congo, and in a wooden canoe she plied the tributaries of the Congo River, trading goods with the natives and collecting fish for the British Museum. She learned the languages of the interior and befriended the local tribes. She became an expert on their rich belief systems, which were completely unknown in Europe. Like many explorers, Mary Kingsley's knowledge bridged separate worlds, helping each understand and appreciate the other.

Gertrude Bell (1868–1926) was the daughter of a wealthy English industrialist. She had tremendous ambition, which she used to convince her parents to give her an education at a time when, for a woman, education was considered secondary to a good marriage. As a result of her intelligence and determination, she won one of the few coveted spots for women at Oxford University. After college, she did not know what to do. Girls of her class usually waited at home for a proposal of marriage. But after Bell returned home, she received an invitation from her uncle to visit Persia (modern-day Iran). Quickly, she set about learning Persian. Later she learned Arabic and begin her own archeological trips into the Syrian deserts.

When World War I broke out, Bell was in the Middle East. Her ability to speak the language, as well as her knowledge of the local tribes and the deserts from her archeological work, caused the British to appoint her to one of the most important jobs in the Desert War, that of Oriental Secretary. The Oriental Secretary was the officer of the embassy who was expected to know about and deal with local affairs, roughly what we call a political officer in an embassy. Bell played a major role in crafting the division of the Middle East into the countries we know today. She also founded the museum in Iraq.

Alexandra David-Néel (1868–1969) was performing in the Paris Opera when she married a banker. As she now had some financial freedom, she decided to act on her lifelong dream to travel to the East. Soon after she married, she sailed alone for India. She assured her husband she be gone only about 18 months; it would be 24 years before she would return home. Upon arriving in India she became intrigued with the Buddhist religion. She felt in order to understand Buddhism, she had first to master Tibetan, the language in which many of the texts were written. In the course of doing so, she plunged so deeply into the culture that she became a Buddhist nun. After several years of study, David-Néel became determined to visit the home of the spiritual leader of the Tibetan Buddhists, the Dalai Lama, who resided in the Holy City of Lhasa, in Tibet. This was quite a challenge because all foreigners were forbidden from entering Lhasa. At the age of 55, she began a long and arduous winter trek across the Himalayas toward Tibet. She succeeded in becoming the first Western woman to visit Lhasa. After returning to France, David-Néel dedicated the rest of her long life to helping Westerners understand the beauty and complexity of Buddhist religion and culture through her many writings.

A wealthy and restless young woman, Annie Montague Alexander (1867–1950) decided to pursue her interests in science and nature rather than live the life of a socialite in San Francisco. She organized numerous expeditions throughout the American West to collect flora, fauna, and fossils. Concerned by the rapid changes occurring due to the growing population, Alexander envisaged a time, all too soon, when much of the natural world of the West would be gone due to urbanization and agricultural development. As a tribute to the land she loved, she decided to create the best natural history museum of the American West. She actually created two museums at the University of California, Berkeley, in which to house the thousands of specimens she had assembled. In the course of her exploration, she discovered new species, seventeen of which are named for her. Though little known, Alexander contributed much to our knowledge of American zoology and paleontology.

Two women in this series are still actively exploring. Sue Hendrickson dropped out of high school and made a living by collecting fish off the Florida Keys to sell to aquariums. An invitation to go on an underwater dive trip changed her life. She became passionate about diving, and soon found herself working with archeologists on wrecks. Hendrickson was often the lead diver, diving first to find out what was there. She realized she had a knack for seeing things others missed. On land, she became an amber collector of pieces of fossilized resin that contained insects and later became a dinosaur hunter. While on a fossil expedition in the Badlands of the Dakotas, Hendrickson discovered the largest *Tyrannosaurus rex* ever found. It has been named Sue in her honor. Depending on the time of year, she can be found diving in the sunken ancient port of Alexandria, Egypt, mapping Spanish wrecks off Cuba's coastline, or in the high, dry lands of ancient forests hunting for dinosaur bones.

Sylvia Earle began her exploration of the sea in the early days of scuba. Smitten with the undersea world, she earned degrees in biology and oceanography. She wanted more than to just study the sea; she wanted to live in the sea. In the early 1970s, Earle was eager to take part in a project in which humans lived in a module underwater for extended periods of time for the U.S. Navy. Unfortunately, when the project was about to begin, she was informed that because she was a woman, she could not go. Undaunted, Earle designed the next phase of the project exclusively for women. This project had far-reaching results. It proved to the U.S. military that women could live well in a confined environment and opened the door for women's entry into the space program.

Earle, ever reaching for new challenges, began designing and testing submersibles, which would allow a human to experience the underwater world more intimately than anything created up to that time. Approaching age 70, her goal is to explore the deepest, darkest place on earth: the 35,800-foot-deep Marianas Trench south of Guam, in the Pacific Ocean.

The experiences of these six women illustrate different paths, different experiences, and different situations, but each led to a similar fulfillment in exploration. All are explorers; all have given us the gift of understanding some aspect of our world. All offer tremendous opportunities to us. Each of us can learn from them and follow in their paths. They are trailblazers; but many trails remain unexplored. There is so much unknown about the world, so much that needs to be understood. For example, less than 5 percent of the ocean has been explored. Thousands of species of plants and animals wait to be discovered. We have not reached every place on earth, and of what we have seen, we often understand very little. Today, we are embarked on the greatest age of exploration. And we go armed with more knowledge than any of the explorers who have gone before us.

What these women teach us is that we need explorers to help us understand what is miraculous in the world around us. The goal for each of us is to find his or her own path and begin the journey.

1

Devoted
to Science

Annie Montague Alexander (1867–1950) might have lived a life of leisure and luxury. Instead, this spirited and hard-driving heir to a Hawaiian sugar fortune chose to pursue a very different path as a naturalist, explorer, farmer, and founder and benefactor of two major research museums at the University of California at Berkeley.

Annie's deep interest in nature stemmed from her childhood years on the Hawaiian island of Maui, where she whiled away countless hours exploring the pristine forests, mountains, and beaches that surrounded her home. After moving to Oakland, California, with her family as a teenager, Annie soon became disgruntled with city life, finding her new role as a genteel young society woman confining and dull. During her twenties, Annie turned to travel as a means of gratifying her restless and inquisitive spirit. Her favorite traveling companion was her father, Samuel Alexander, who encouraged Annie's passion for adventure and the great out-of-doors.

Following the death of her beloved father while he was on safari with her in East Africa, however, Annie felt compelled to do something more with her life—and her substantial inheritance—than merely indulge her thirst for adventure through globetrotting. In 1907, three years after Samuel's fatal accident, Annie hit upon the idea of founding a natural history museum at the University of California at Berkeley, a few miles from her home in Oakland.

Educating and entertaining the public through exhibitions of preserved and mounted animals such as those featured in the popular Field Museum of Natural History in Chicago or American Museum of Natural History in New York City was not Alexander's goal in founding a museum. Rather, Alexander wanted her facility to be a center of scientific research, devoted to preserving, describing, and studying specimens of the western United States' diverse wildlife, which was already vanishing by the early twentieth century.

Yet, Annie Montague Alexander wanted to do more than merely provide the financial backing for the Museum of Vertebrate Zoology, as her new institution came to be known. (Zoology is the branch of biology that deals with animals; vertebrates are animals that possess a backbone or spinal column.) After the Museum of Vertebrate Zoology officially opened its doors in 1909, Annie devoted the remaining four decades of her life to actively building its collections and research programs, taking dozens of field trips throughout California and western North America in search of zoological specimens. With the indispensable assistance of her long-time collecting partner and fellow amateur naturalist, Louise Kellogg, Alexander amassed nearly 23,000 vertebrate specimens for the museum, primarily small mammals but also birds, reptiles, and amphibians.

In addition to their zoological fieldwork, Annie Alexander and Louise Kellogg collected some 1,500 fossil specimens from sites across the western United States for the Museum of Paleontology at Berkeley. (Paleontology is the study of early life forms based on fossil remains.) Created in 1874, the Museum of Paleontology was part of the university's geology and paleontology departments for nearly 50 years. Eager to advance paleontological research at Berkeley, in 1921 Alexander financed and organized the University of California Museum of Paleontology as a completely independent research unit within the school.

Fascinated by all aspects of the natural world, during the final decade of her long and remarkably productive life, Alexander switched her focus from animals, recent or extinct, to plants. Together with Louise Kellogg, Annie gathered nearly 18,000 botanical specimens from the western United States and Mexico for yet another University of California research institution, the University herbarium. (Botany is the branch of biology that deals with plants; a herbarium is a collection of dried and mounted plant specimens that are systematically arranged.)

In biological fieldwork, Alexander managed to carve out for herself "a career of adventure . . . redeemed by its scientific prospects," as she once put it.[1] Field collecting for the University herbarium and the zoological and paleontological museums that she founded at Berkeley allowed Annie to satisfy two of her most fundamental spiritual and psychological needs: to

ZOOLOGICAL FIELDWORK: From Collecting Specimens to Observing Live Animals

When Annie Montague Alexander began collecting specimens for the Museum of Vertebrate Zoology, the primary emphasis in zoological fieldwork was on obtaining and preserving specimens, or "study specimens" as they were called, to be classified, described, and examined in detail by scientists in museums and other research institutions far removed from the field. Yet while the custom of trapping and shooting animals in order to study their preserved carcasses remained prevalent within zoological fieldwork throughout Annie Alexander's long life, by the early twentieth century, more and more naturalists and scientists were beginning to engage in a very different sort of fieldwork. This type of fieldwork centered on closely observing live animals in their natural habitats, typically over extended periods.

One scientist of Alexander's era who adopted this approach was the pioneering female ornithologist Florence Merriam Bailey. Rather than shooting birds and preparing specimens of their skins like Alexander and other traditional field collectors, Bailey focused on observing and describing the animals' behavior in the wild, sometimes watching for many hours at a time as a bird cared for its young or fashioned a nest. Over the course of the twentieth century, Florence Merriam Bailey's method of observing live animals in their natural settings would gradually replace the collecting of study specimens as the chief focus of zoological fieldwork.

achieve something of lasting value during her time on earth and to spend as much of that time as possible adventuring in the great outdoors. This included trekking across vast, lonely deserts in Nevada, scaling lofty mountain peaks in California, or exploring the uncharted interior of a remote Alaskan island. In an age when scientific careers were all but closed to females, and few women worked outside their homes, Annie Montague Alexander took as her life's calling the promotion of scientific knowledge. She did this through organizing and funding two world-renowned museums, and collecting tens of thousands of animal, fossil, and plant specimens that would lay the foundation for decades of important research in zoology, paleontology, botany, ecology, and a host of other scientific fields.

2

An Island
Childhood

Annie Montague Alexander was born in Honolulu, Hawaii, on December 29, 1867. Her parents, Samuel and Martha Cooke Alexander, were the children of missionaries who had come to the Hawaiian Archipelago all the way from New England to convert its "heathen" inhabitants to their Protestant Christian faith.

ANNIE'S MISSIONARY HERITAGE

In 1831 Annie's paternal grandfather, the Reverend William Patterson Alexander, and his wife of just one month, Mary Ann McKinney Alexander, boarded a sailing ship in the port of New Bedford, Massachusetts, and bid farewell to their families and native country forever. Twenty-six-year-old William and his twenty-one-year-old bride were bound for an exotic tropical paradise a half a world away from home—the Hawaiian Islands (or Sandwich Islands, as they were then known).

Along with eight other couples, the Alexanders were traveling to Hawaii under the auspices of a Boston-based evangelical organization, the American Board of Commissioners for Foreign Missions (ABCFM). The ABCFM had started sending small "companies" or "packets" of Protestant ministers, teachers, printers, and doctors from New England to Hawaii a decade earlier, to bring both Christianity and American culture to the islands. The Alexanders were part of the fifth ABCFM packet; over the next two decades, the organization would send seven more companies to the island kingdom. The determined little bands of Yankee evangelists faced an arduous voyage that might last anywhere from four to eight months and entailed sailing down South America's Atlantic coast all the way to the continent's notorious tip at Cape Horn. After making the perilous journey around the Cape with its mountainous waves and frigid winds, the voyagers then pushed northwestward through the Pacific to the remote Hawaiian Archipelago.

By the time that the Alexanders arrived in Hawaii, a decade of energetic missionary activity by the ABCFM had secured a strong foothold for Christianity on the archipelago and brought numerous changes in the day-to-day lives of its inhabitants. Grimly determined to root out "heathenish" social customs and religious practices, the missionaries prodded Hawaiians to adopt more modest, New-England style attire, as well as American legal and moral codes. In their campaign to overthrow traditional Hawaiian beliefs and customs, the missionaries were greatly aided by the islands' rulers. Just months before the first ABCFM company arrived in 1820, Hawaii's new monarch officially abandoned many of the central *kapus* (taboos) of the kingdom's ancient religious system, thereby creating a spiritual vacuum on the archipelago and preparing the way for the Yankee evangelists.

The Alexanders' first assignment in their new homeland was on Kauai, the most northerly of the eight major islands in the Hawaiian Archipelago. At the tiny community of Waioli, they constructed a two-story, New England–style mission house of coral limestone blocks and set out to teach the islanders Christian doctrine along with the rudiments of reading and writing. Since as Calvinist Protestants they believed each person must study the Scriptures for himself or herself, the ABCFM missionaries placed great emphasis on promoting literacy among the Hawaiian people. In teaching their little flock at Waioli to read, the Alexanders undoubtedly used the 12-letter Hawaiian alphabet devised by the first ABCFM company. After discovering the islanders possessed no written language, the early missionaries promptly invented one for them, and then printed up Hawaiian-language bibles by the thousands for distribution throughout the archipelago.

SAMUEL ALEXANDER: ANNIE'S RESTLESS FATHER

After spending 12 years on Kauai, the Alexanders were reassigned to Maui, the second largest island in the archipelago, where William had been granted the prestigious post of director of the Lahainaluna Seminary. Situated on a picturesque hillside overlooking the bustling port of Lahaina, the seminary's chief purpose was to train native boys to work among their people as teachers and ministers. Founded by ABCFM missionaries in 1831 and patterned after a New England "normal" or teacher training school, Lahainaluna is generally credited with being the first American secondary school west of the Rocky Mountains.

By the time William and Mary Ann settled in Lahaina in 1843, they were the parents of five young children, including Annie's father, Samuel Thomas, then a lively and adventuresome seven-year-old. Like his minister father, who planted dozens of fruit and shade trees near the family home at Lahaina, young Samuel delighted in nature. On foot or on horseback, Samuel spent many contented hours exploring the sparkling waterfalls, palm-fringed beaches, verdant forests, and soaring mountains of his western Maui home. Samuel's frequent companion on these excursions was his best friend, Henry Baldwin, the son of another New England missionary stationed in Lahaina.

In keeping with his New England Puritan heritage, Reverend Alexander placed a high value on education and learning. Thus, when Samuel was in his early teens, William sent him to the island of Oahu to attend the Punahou School, a Honolulu boarding school designed to prepare missionaries' children for college back in the United States, usually in New England. Following his graduation from Punahou, however, Samuel did not head for Massachusetts or Connecticut to earn his college degree. Instead, he decided to go to Kauai, the island of his birth, to serve a one-year internship as a merchant and bookkeeper on a sugar plantation.

By 1854, when Samuel started his internship, sugar was well on its way to becoming the chief export of the Hawaiian Archipelago. Barely two decades earlier, an enterprising New Englander had established the first successful sugar plantation on the islands. Since then, the market for Hawaiian sugar had expanded rapidly in the United States, Hawaii's central trading partner. Hawaiian sugar sold particularly well in the new state of California, whose population had mushroomed since gold was discovered on John Sutter's land in the Sacramento Valley in 1848, and which was just a 14-day voyage away from the islands.

By the end of his internship, Samuel's aptitude for both business and farming was evident. Yet, with the islands in the midst of a temporary economic downturn in 1855, his employment prospects looked bleak. Eager to see more of the world and lured by the prospect of making a quick fortune, 19-year-old Samuel resolved to head for California to try his luck in the gold fields. By the mid-1850s, however, a flood of gold seekers from all over the United States and the world had already mined dry the state's more accessible gold deposits. Although Samuel was more than willing to work hard for what he desired—"he has more *go ahead* than any of my sons"—the Reverend Alexander once said of his third-born, after a year of backbreaking toil and a bout with malaria (a debilitating illness spread by mosquitoes), Samuel was ready to give up on his Californian adventure.[2]

Having spent what little money he had been able to earn from gold mining on his medical care, Samuel was flat broke when he arrived back home in Maui. Although he had never shown an interest in teaching before, Samuel now decided to pursue a teaching career at Lahainaluna Seminary, undoubtedly at the urging of his father, the principal. To qualify as an instructor, however, Samuel needed more schooling himself. Thus, he soon embarked on his second trip to the United States, this time journeying all the way to Massachusetts, where he studied for two years at Williams College.

Back at Lahainaluna, since the seminary emphasized the teaching of practical skills in addition to traditional academic courses, Samuel decided to put the knowledge he had acquired during his Kauai internship to good use by having his students raise sugarcane and other food crops on school land. Samuel's agricultural endeavors at Lahainaluna proved so successful that he soon came to the attention of a sugar plantation owner at Waihee in northern Maui. When the plantation owner offered him a position as his operations manager, eager for a new challenge, Samuel quickly accepted.

IN THE SHADOW OF HALEAKALA

Shortly after taking the position in Waihee, Samuel married his longtime fiancee, Martha Cooke, whose parents had sailed to Hawaii from New England with the eighth company of ABCFM missionaries. Within three years of their wedding in 1864, the couple had two daughters and one son: Juliette, Annie Montague, and Wallace. Eventually, Samuel and Martha would have two more children: Martha, born in 1878, and Clarence, who would die in 1884, shortly before his fourth birthday.

Though he now had a family to support, Samuel was too restless to stay in one spot or at one job for long. Samuel explained in a letter to his brother William in 1866:

> What is the use of settling down comfortably and lead-ing a good virtuous and industrious life and then dying? No, I would rather start off in quest of the elixir of life, and roam ragged and hungry over barren mountain summits, than live the life of the most virtuous and useful men.[3]

Hence, not quite four years after settling in Waihee, Samuel resigned his position at the plantation and moved his family to the little town of Haiku in north-central Maui, where he intended to launch a bold new venture. Samuel had resolved to establish his own sugarcane plantation on several hundred acres of land he had recently purchased with his new business partner and best friend from his childhood years in Lahaina, Henry Baldwin.

The two young men had been able to afford the land for their sugarcane plantation for one reason and one alone: its awful location. The property sat directly in the rain shadow of Haleakala, reputed to be the world's largest dormant volcano. Towering more than 10,000 feet above sea level with a crater basin at its summit so vast it could contain all of Manhattan Island, Haleakala dominates the entire eastern half of Maui. Because of its tremendous bulk, the volcano significantly affects weather patterns throughout the island. The Pacific's famous trade winds (steady breezes that flow from the northeast through the east) carry copious rain clouds along with them. On Maui's lushly vegetated windward coast, the moisture-laden

THE EXTRAORDINARY HALEAKALA

The volcano that dominated the landscape of Annie's childhood on Maui had an important place in ancient Hawaiian religion. In Hawaiian, *Haleakala* means "House of the Sun" and according to legend the volcano's summit was where the demigod Maui lassoed the sun to slow down its journey across the sky and provide islanders with more daylight hours for fishing or drying tapa (a traditional cloth made from tree bark).

Composed of very dense, hardened lava that has been compared to poured cement, Haleakala reaches 30,000 feet below the ocean and 10,023 feet above sea level. Scientists believe that Haleakala, the larger of two volcanoes that fused to form the island of Maui, first thrust itself out of the ocean some 800,000 years ago. Surprisingly, it was hundreds of years of erosion, rather than volcanic activity, that hollowed out the seven-mile wide, half-mile deep crater at Haleakala's summit, where temperatures are typically 30 degrees lower than at sea level. The most recent volcanic activity at Haleakala was a flank eruption, and occurred more than winds dump more than 100 inches of precipitation a year in some spots. Since giant Haleakala effectively blocks the breezes, however, comparatively little rain falls on the mountain's leeward (western) side, where Alexander and Baldwin's new fields were located.

Nonetheless, anxious to take advantage of the rising demand for Hawaiian sugar in California and the rest of the United States, the partners were willing to take their chances on cultivating sugarcane, a plant that requires an abundant and steady supply of water, in Haleakala's long, arid shadow. Undoubtedly, the two were aware of the irrigation project recently undertaken on the Kaui sugar plantation where Samuel

two centuries ago. Nonetheless, Haleakala is classified as a dormant rather than an extinct volcano, meaning that scientists believe there is a real possibility it may erupt again at some point in the future.

During Annie's childhood, silversword grew abundantly on the plateau-like floor of Haleakala's crater. However, by the mid-twentieth century, the beautiful silver-leafed plant had all but disappeared from Maui, having been gobbled by wild goats or picked by the increasing numbers of tourists who now made their way to Haleakala's summit. In 1961, Haleakala's vast summit was finally declared a national park and today, under the watchful eye of park rangers, silversword is making a dramatic comeback along with another endangered Hawaiian native, the nene. In 1946, hunters, predators, and disease had reduced the islands' entire nene population to less than 50. Now, following a government-sponsored breeding program, the number of nene geese at Haleakala National Park stands at close to 300.

had interned as a teenager. Following a lengthy drought, Alexander's former boss, William Rice, had constructed a ten-mile-long system of ditches and pipes to collect water from nearby mountainside streams and convey it to his parched fields. Although Samuel and Henry had no background in engineering, by 1876, with their sugar acreage expanding and their water shortage becoming ever more acute, the partners decided the time had come to launch an irrigation project of their own.

These two ministers' sons approached their difficult under-taking with a missionary-like zeal. With painstaking precision, they contrived a system of open ditches and tunnels capable of gathering and transporting millions of gallons of water from rivulets and streams on Haleakala's windward side. In just two years, with the indispensable assistance of native Hawaiian laborers, Alexander and Baldwin had built an irrigation system twice the length of the one that Rice had constructed on Kaui. Winding across deep ravines and through steep ridges, the new aqueduct swept enough water down the mountainside to irrigate thousands of acres of thirsty sugarcane.

The irrigation system combined with the brand new Reciprocity Treaty between Hawaii and the United States, which eliminated all taxes on Hawaiian sugar imported to the mainland, secured the future of Alexander and Baldwin's fledgling enterprise. Over the next few years, the two bought up more and more land in north-central Maui. To work their steadily expanding acreage, in common with the other *haole* (Caucasian) sugar barons on the archipelago, Alexander and Baldwin relied primarily on imported labor, particularly from Asia. Native Hawaiians, the haole landowners had discovered, were considerably less willing than the new immigrants to toil long hours for meager pay. Besides, by the late 1800s, the islands' native population had been severely depleted by smallpox, measles, and other viruses introduced to the once isolated archipelago by foreign sailors and missionaries.

ANNIE'S OUT-OF-DOORS CHILDHOOD

While her father devoted himself to building up his new sugar-cane plantation, Annie was enjoying what she would later remember as a nearly idyllic childhood in the Maui countryside. A tomboy to the core, Annie was an avid tree climber and delighted in accessing her bedroom, not by the conventional route via the indoor staircase, but by scaling the roof of the verandah and entering through her window. Naturally athletic and brimming with energy, Annie adored hiking, horseback riding, and swimming. Since her house at Haiku was only a short walk from the ocean, she went often to the seashore to play in the waves and on the sun-drenched beach.

Annie's most cherished childhood memories centered not on Haiku or the ocean, however, but on majestic and mysterious Haleakala. Some 4,000 feet up on the volcano's slopes, the family maintained a summer home in the village of Olinda. There the temperatures were cooler and the air sweeter than down in dusty Haiku. The vegetation and animal life was also more abundant and diverse in the Upcountry, as Haleakala's damp, verdant slopes are generally known, and Annie delighted in the natural wonders that surrounded her at Olinda. Just as her father had devoted countless hours to investigating the wild places around Lahaina as a child, Annie happily whiled away entire days on the mountainside's lushly wooded slopes. From early on, Annie displayed a passion for collecting unusual plant and animal specimens, particularly the colorful and remarkably varied land snails and delicate, emerald-green ferns that flourished on the damp forest floors of Maui.

On cool summer nights, the Alexanders often built bonfires on the mountainside. Pretending she was a genie just released from its lamp, Annie would stand in the thick smoke until her brown hair reeked and her eyes stung, acting out her favorite scenes from the *Arabian Nights*. On other summer evenings, Annie and her siblings rode mules or horses to the very top of Haleakala. After a night spent sleeping under the stars, the children awoke early to watch the sunrise from the volcano's 10,000-foot high summit, a dazzling interplay of light and clouds that today draws thousands of tourists to Haleakala each year.

Before making the long trek back down the mountainside, with her deep appreciation for Hawaii's natural secrets, Annie would undoubtedly have spent time exploring the remarkable 3,000 foot-deep basin at Haleakala's summit. A line of nine symmetrical cinder cones ranging in height from 600 to 1,000 feet crisscross the colorful field of volcanic ash that comprises the crater's vast floor, creating an eerie, lunarlike landscape. In the crater's rough cinder terrain, the budding young naturalist would probably have made a point of searching out the celebrated silversword. This six-foot-tall, silver-leafed plant blooms just once during its 20-year life span, sprouting an enormous stalk of red-purple flowers before wilting and shriveling into a brittle gray skeleton. Extremely rare, the plant grows virtually no place else in the world except on Haleakala's bowl-shaped summit. On her excursions up Haleakala, Annie would also have likely encountered another famous resident of the volcano: the Hawaiian goose, or nene. Believed to be a descendant of the Canada goose, in stark contrast to its North American cousins, the nene makes its home far from the water, nesting high up on the cliffs of Haleakala and a handful of other volcanoes on the Big Island.

LEAVING HOME

In 1881, when she was 13, Annie embarked on a new adventure that promised to be very different from her carefree treks to the summit of Haleakala. That fall, Annie's parents enrolled her at Punahou School, the same secondary school that Samuel Alexander had attended in Hawaii's capital city some three decades earlier. Annie had never attended a regular school before: a live-in governess had taught her and her siblings their lessons in the Alexanders' home at Haiku.

Far from being apprehensive about leaving her home and family, Annie was thrilled by the prospect of the 90-mile-long sea voyage from Maui to Honolulu. Although the independent teenager adjusted quickly to her new life at boarding school, Annie's happiness at Punahou was to prove fleeting. In 1883, to Annie's profound dismay, Samuel Alexander announced that the family would be leaving Hawaii for the U.S. mainland, where they were to take up residence across the bay from San Francisco in the bustling city of Oakland, California.

3

Student
of Nature

Samuel Alexander's desire to forsake the country of his birth for Oakland, California, seems to have been motivated in part by his concerns for his five children, who ranged in age from 3 to 17 years old in 1883. Oakland is nestled along San Francisco Bay, an area celebrated for its cleansing ocean breezes and mild temperatures, which seldom rise above 75 degrees Fahrenheit even in July or August. Samuel considered the Bay area's temperate climate "invigorating," promoting good health and stamina among the local population. In contrast, Alexander believed central Maui's hot climate to be "debilitating," harmful to an individual's moral health as well as his or her physical well-being. The "tendency" of Haiku's oppressive heat, Samuel insisted, was to encourage "sloth [laziness] and vice" among the area's residents.[4]

Not only was the Bay area's moderate climate more conducive to the development of physically and morally sound youngsters than the sultry climate of Maui, but Alexander was convinced there was something about California that inspired self-reliance, a traditional pioneer virtue that Samuel deeply admired. "There is perhaps no country in the world better calculated to develop independence of character than California," Samuel asserted in a letter to his older brother, perhaps recalling his own experiences in the state years earlier as a 19-year-old gold prospector.[5]

THE ALEXANDERS' IMPROVING FORTUNES

Relocating to California undoubtedly appealed to Samuel from a business as well as from a personal perspective. It made sense for Alexander and Baldwin to have one partner stationed on the mainland, the chief market for the firm's sugarcane. From his new home, Samuel could better track developments in the nation's capital regarding tariffs on Hawaiian sugar, which sugar growers on the mainland had fought to have reinstated ever since the Reciprocity Treaty of 1875 removed them, and the controversial issue of American annexation of the islands.

By the 1880s, Hawaii's sugar growers, most of who were of American descent, were concluding that United States annexation of Hawaii was in their best interests. In 1898, the sugar barons and other haole planters and businesspeople in the islands would achieve a long-standing goal when Hawaii was officially incorporated into the United States. Hawaii would remain a U.S. territory for the next six decades until finally attaining statehood in 1959.

In the meantime, the firm of Alexander & Baldwin was prospering and expanding, both on Maui, where the company continued to buy up more land for sugarcane fields, and in San Francisco, where Samuel oversaw the creation of the partners' first American purchasing agency. Soon, the enterprising missionaries' sons had acquired a steamship line to transport their raw sugar the approximately 2,000 miles from Maui to San Francisco and had established their first sugar refinery in the northern California town of Crockett, where the well-known C & H (Californian and Hawaiian) brand of table sugar is still produced today.

With his sugar and shipping businesses booming, Samuel Alexander could afford to have a large and elegant house built for his family in one of Oakland's most exclusive neighborhoods. Although they had opted not to reside in San Francisco, preferring to raise their family in the more sedate community of Oakland, Samuel and Martha took full advantage of the larger city's cultural amenities, frequently making the brief ferry trip across the Bay to attend the theater, symphony, or opera.

Her parents might appreciate their adopted home's social and cultural opportunities, but Annie missed Hawaii's free and easy atmosphere and found her new existence as a member of the Bay area's "upper crust" confining. Whereas Martha Cooke Alexander seems to have thoroughly enjoyed her new role as a fashionable Oakland matron, Annie had little use for her mother's high-society world. Still a tomboy at heart, Annie felt painfully out of place at the seemingly endless round of dinners, balls, and other genteel entertainment an affluent young woman of the era was expected to attend. Even relatively informal social functions such as teas left Annie feeling uneasy and inadequate. "You already know my sentiment about teas," Annie wrote to a friend. "I always feel the masquerader among the masked." [6]

AN EDUCATED FEMALE

In the fall of 1887 when Annie was 19, Samuel and Martha Alexander decided to send their restless second child east to continue her education. Annie would attend the Lasell Seminary for Young Women, a junior college in Auburndale, Massachusetts. At Lasell, she would join a close childhood friend from Maui, Mary Beckwith, whose grandparents had also been missionaries with the ABCFM.

Parents who encouraged daughters to continue their education beyond secondary school were viewed as progressive in their attitudes toward women in the nineteenth century. Many people still clung to the old notion that an advanced degree was a wasteful luxury for girls whose chief end in life was presumed to be marriage, motherhood, and keeping house. Moreover, it was commonly believed that extensive intellectual training was not only superfluous for girls but also injurious to them. Supposedly, serious study overstrained the "fragile" female body and brain. In the 1870s, this attitude toward girls and book learning received "scientific" backing from a Boston physician named Edward Clarke. Clarke's highly publicized book, *Sex in Education*, blasted the growing trend among middle- and upper-class young women to enroll in two-year academies or "seminaries" such as Lasell after high school or even worse, at full-fledged, four-year colleges and universities. Long hours in the classroom and grueling late night study sessions, the doctor warned, would consume the young female's already "limited energy," leaving her vulnerable to a host of ills ranging from "uterine disease" to "hysteria, and other derangements of the nervous system."[7]

The issue of women and advanced learning was still being hotly debated throughout the western world in the late 1800s, but statistics indicate that a rising number of American parents like the Alexanders were coming to the conclusion that more benefit than harm would come to their daughters through a post-secondary education. According to the historian Barbara Solomon, during the last three decades of the nineteenth century, the number of females enrolled in institutions of higher learning in the United States increased nearly eight-fold, from 11,000, or approximately 20 percent of the total college population, in 1870, to 85,000, or about 35 percent of all post-secondary school students, in 1900.

A DIVERSE CURRICULUM

At the Lasell Seminary for Young Women, Annie's diverse studies included Roman history, English literature, logic, French, German, and photography. She took only one stereo-typically feminine class—dress cutting, which was offered by the school's "Domestic Science Department" along with courses in cooking, china-painting, and "art-needlework."[8] Despite her deep childhood interest in natural history, there is no indication that Alexander enrolled in any science classes during the two years that she spent at Lasell, though botany, geology, chemistry, and other science courses had been offered at the seminary since its establishment in 1851.

With its varied and demanding academic curriculum, it is evident that Lasell was much more than just a "finishing school" (a school where girls from affluent families were often sent to learn the rules of proper etiquette and how to be charming in society).

Nonetheless, since most professions, with the exception of teaching, remained closed to women until well into the twentieth century, Lasell Seminary emphasized self-development and personal enrichment rather than professional training for its students. As the historian Margaret W. Rossiter points out, a hundred years ago, "hardly anyone expected middle-class women to, or wanted them to, hold jobs outside the home," regardless of whether they continued their education beyond secondary school.[9]

"PHYSICAL CULTURE" AND MILITARY DRILLS

An important component of the Lasell program was "physical culture," which is what we know as physical education today. [10] Every morning before their regular classes started, Annie and her schoolmates were required to participate in organized calisthenics. Influenced by the popular health reform movement of the nineteenth century, educators throughout the United States emphasized the intimate connection between healthy minds and healthy bodies. Consequently, some type of organized physical exercise was compulsory for students at virtually all colleges and universities of the era. Communal calisthenics was a particularly common form of physical activity for female scholars. Often accompanied by music, these exercise routines were designed to provide young women with a moderate physical workout while at the same time promoting grace of movement and correct posture.

In 1888, during Annie's second year at Lasell, the school's physical education program expanded and became significantly more rigorous when a "natatorium" (swimming pool) was constructed on campus and all students were required to learn how to swim. By the late 1880s, more strenuous athletic programs, including rowing, swimming, and tennis were beginning to gain acceptance at other women's schools as well, as new ideas regarding women's health and physical capabilities began to take hold and long accepted ones regarding "ladylike" versus "unladylike" activities came to be viewed as old-fashioned.

Yet, if the Lasell Seminary's growing emphasis on more rigorous athletic instruction was in keeping with national trends, the school's adoption of a paramilitary drill regime for its female pupils was truly innovative. In 1888, the same year that the swimming pool was installed, Annie and her classmates began attending compulsory military drills twice weekly under the instruction of a U.S. Army major who lived in Auburndale. Similar to the paramilitary exercises practiced at many men's academies and colleges of the day, the maneuvers were meant to promote discipline, patriotism, and good posture among the young women of Lasell. The students were outfitted with special military-style uniforms (featuring ankle-length skirts rather than trousers), visored caps adorned with the insignia LSB (for Lasell Seminary Battalion), and wooden rifles. At the end of the school year, the Lasell battalion put on a demonstration for the community that attracted big crowds and the attention of the local press. There is no record of Annie's feelings about this unusual program, but there is evidence that the military exercises were a popular component of Lasell's curriculum. Indeed, the school would continue the drills for another three decades before finally abandoning the program after World War I (1914–18).

SEARCHING FOR A PATH

In the spring of 1889, having completed two years of study at Lasell, 21-year-old Annie departed Auburndale with no clear conception of what she wanted to do next. On a family vacation to Europe the following summer, she hit upon the idea of staying on in Paris to study painting and drawing, for which she showed some natural talent. Taking up residence with an aunt who lived in the city, Annie attended art classes at the prestigious Sorbonne. After a few months, however, she began suffering from persistent eyestrain and excruciating headaches. Annie consulted one specialist after another. To her dismay, they all agreed that her vision problems and headaches would almost certainly worsen if she continued to perform the close work demanded of an art student. Deeply disappointed, Annie returned to Oakland and moved back into her parents' house.

Shortly after arriving home, Annie decided to enroll in a training program for prospective nurses at a local hospital. Annie was not seeking a means of supporting herself: her father's substantial wealth and unfailing generosity toward his adult offspring meant that she would never have to earn her own daily bread. Yet, as she approached her mid-twenties, Annie felt that she needed some sort of regular work to fill her days and give her a sense of purpose, and nursing, along with teaching, was one of the few careers open to females in the late 1800s. To Annie's consternation, however, studying the required medical texts soon brought on a recurrence of the severe headaches and eyestrain that had plagued her in Paris, and she was compelled to give up her dream of nursing just as she had had to relinquish her artistic ambitions.

In her quest to give her existence meaning and direction, Annie appears to have never seriously considered marriage and motherhood, although caring for a husband and children was generally deemed a woman's greatest purpose in life until well into the twentieth century. Indeed, single women typically received scant respect in American society during Annie's youth. An unmarried woman over the age of 25 or so could expect to be saddled with the unflattering labels of "old maid" or "spinster" and was commonly viewed with contempt or pity, or both, by her community. Nonetheless, there is no indication that Annie ever regretted her unmarried status. On the contrary, Annie seems to have feared that the demands of marriage and motherhood would consume too much of her time and energy and rob her of her independence. "I saw Mary McLean Olney this morning," Annie noted dryly in a letter to a female friend. "She was dean of Pomona College for a year, liked the work and would have enjoyed going on with it had not this other thing come up—that of falling in love and getting married."[11] Although at this point in time, Annie's "purpose in life may have been unclear," writes Alexander's biographer, Barbara Stein, "she instinctively recognized that marriage would not quell her restlessness and pervasive malaise [a feeling of psychological uneasiness]." [12]

Frustrated in her efforts to establish a career for herself in art or nursing, in her late twenties Annie turned to travel as an outlet for her considerable energies. Her chief traveling companion during this period was her father, an insatiable globetrotter who spent a substantial portion of his newfound wealth on visiting such far-flung places as Iceland, Australia, Egypt, Scotland, and Peru. Annie and Samuel made ideal traveling partners: both were restless spirits who craved novel adventures and reveled in physical challenges. During the 1890s, Annie and her father enjoyed several lengthy trips together, including a voyage to Asia and the South Pacific with stops in China, Japan, New Zealand and the Samoan Islands and a three-month-long bicycling tour through France, Switzerland, and England, during which they managed to peddle 1,500 miles.

CAMPING OUT

In 1899, Annie embarked on a trip that was destined to forever change her life. On this excursion, her companion would not be her father but rather Martha Beckwith, the younger sister of her childhood friend and fellow Lasell alumni, Mary Beckwith. Martha, a graduate of Mount Holyoke College, had taught at several women's colleges in New England, including her alma mater. Although she would eventually earn a master's degree from Columbia University in anthropology (the science that focuses on the origins and customs of humankind), Beckwith loved all aspects of the natural world and had a particular interest in botany, ornithology, and geology. (Ornithology is the branch of zoology that deals with birds; geology deals with the history of the Earth, especially as recorded in its rocks.) In the spring of 1899, while on a visit to the West Coast, Martha invited Annie to go camping with her. Beckwith proposed an itinerary that would take the two women through the rugged

Camping was a popular pastime in the late 1800s, and Annie took her first trip to the wilderness with a friend at the age of 31. She immediately loved exploring and analyzing the species and specimens they found. One highlight of their trip was the majestic landscapes of the Cascade Mountains, including the dormant volcano Mount Shasta, seen here.

wilderness of northern California and southern Oregon as far north as Crater Lake. Along the way, they would collect interesting plants, shoot photographs, bird watch, and just drink in the spectacular scenery.

By the late nineteenth century, camping had emerged as a popular American pastime, especially for the urban middle class. As early as 1874, notes the historian Donna Braden, the national periodical *Scribners Monthly* reported "'camping out' was rapidly growing in favor, providing city dwellers with temporary relief from artificiality and confinement." [13] Interestingly, camping out was not perceived as a male-only form of recreation: many American women and girls enthusiastically participated in the "back-to-nature" movement of the late 1800s. What was unusual about Annie and Martha's expedition, however, considering the prevailing attitudes of their era, was that they would be two women traveling and camping alone, without the benefit of a man's protection or guidance. Whether Annie's parents approved of her rather daring excursion is unknown, but there is no indication that they made any effort to prevent the trip. They may have figured that at age 31 Annie ought to be permitted to make her own decisions, even though she still lived under their roof.

EXPEDITION TO CRATER LAKE

In late May 1899, Annie and Martha set out on horseback for what turned out to be a 10-week, 600-mile-long trek. When the weather was unusually chilly or wet, they might ride to the nearest town and spend the night at an inn, but most nights the women slept under the stars, unrolling their blankets onto crude beds they had fashioned from pine or tamarack boughs. As they traveled northward, the pair hunted for unusual plant specimens, took many pictures with the bulky photographic equipment they had resolutely dragged along with them, and bird watched—with Martha diligently teaching Annie the names of all the different birds they spotted.

Crossing the border into Oregon, Annie and Martha stopped at Klamath Falls, then made their way to the crest of the Cascade Mountain range and Crater Lake. Famed for its exquisite sapphire-blue waters, Crater Lake lies inside a gigantic basin formed some 8,000 years ago when the top of the 12,000-feet-high volcano Mount Mazama collapsed following an eruption. Over time, the crater filled with water to become the deepest lake in the United States.

Heading back into California, Annie and Martha marveled at another natural wonder of the Cascade Range: lofty, snow-crested Mount Shasta. Viewing the dormant volcano silhouetted against the brilliant reds and oranges of the setting sun, the two women later agreed, was the single most thrilling moment of their journey. Another highlight of the women's trip home was their three-hour-long hike to the summit of Lassens Peak, a 10,457-feet-high inactive volcano at the southernmost end of the Cascade Range.

Annie treasured every minute of her ten-week-long sojourn with Martha into the wilds of northern California and southern Oregon. Spending her days in the midst of majestic mountain ranges and vast, untouched forests and meadows, and her nights sleeping beneath a canopy of stars was Annie's idea of heaven on earth. No doubt, she would have concurred with John Muir, the great American naturalist and conservationist of the late nineteenth century, regarding the restorative power of the wilderness: "Everybody needs beauty as well as bread," Muir wrote, "places to play in and pray in, where nature may heal and cheer and give strength to body and soul."[14]

Yet Annie's two months in the mountains with Beckwith did more than merely soothe and strengthen her "body and soul": it also left her with exciting new intellectual interests. Alexander had delighted in learning about the natural history of the American West from Martha, who, taking all of nature as her classroom, shared with her friend everything that she knew about the rocks, birds, and plants that they encountered along their way.

A PASSION FOR NATURE

By the end of the expedition, Annie had discovered her life's passion—the natural world. Without the guidance of her friend Martha, who had departed for the East Coast to assume a teaching position immediately after their trip's conclusion, however, Annie seemed bewildered as to how to pursue her compelling new scientific interests. A year after their trip to Crater Lake, faced with the prospect of a long, lonely winter while her parents traveled abroad, Annie persuaded Martha to take a hiatus from teaching and spend a few months with her at her family's home in Oakland. During her visit, Martha encouraged Annie to broaden her knowledge of the natural world by auditing a science class at the University of California in Berkeley, only a short distance away from Oakland.

Spurred on by Martha, in the fall of 1900 Annie decided to audit a course in paleontology taught by John C. Merriam, a popular lecturer and respected researcher in the study of the earth's earliest life forms. Thus began what would turn out to be a five-decade-long relationship between Annie Montague Alexander and the University of California at Berkeley, a relationship that would prove exceptionally fruitful to both of them.

4

Hunting for Fossils and Big Game

From the start, Annie Alexander was captivated by John Merriam's lectures on paleontology, particularly by the professor's accounts of his own fossil hunting expeditions in California and Oregon. "But what a fever the study of old Earth that you thought should be a part of my education has set up in me!" Annie wrote happily to Martha Beckwith. "I am really alarmed," she teased. "If it were a general interest in geology there might be something quite wholesome in it but it seems to centralize on fossils, fossils! And I am beleaguered." [15]

Despite her enthusiasm for paleontology and natural history generally, Alexander never enrolled at the University of California as a regular student. Her hesitancy to enter a degree program probably had nothing to do with her gender: the number of female students at Berkeley, as at other state universities around the country, rose dramatically during the last decade of the nineteenth century and first decade of the twentieth century. By 1910, reports the historian Barbara Solomon, nearly 40 percent of the total student body at American colleges and universities was female. Furthermore, by the start of the twentieth century, graduate as well as undergraduate programs had been opened to females at most universities across the nation, including the University of California, so that women could now pursue the same doctorates in science and other disciplines as men.

It seems likely that Alexander's decision to merely audit courses at the university rather than take them for credit was linked to her ongoing concerns about her eyesight. Studying long hours for tests, she may have worried, might cause a recurrence of the severe eyestrain and headaches that had plagued her in Paris and during her brief stint as a nursing student. In addition to her apprehensions regarding her eyesight, Alexander also evidently harbored doubts regarding her academic abilities. Annie openly admired the intellectual talents of others, including her best friend, Martha Beckwith, but believed herself to be somehow lacking as a student. "I stand aghast when I am brought face to face with what a real student accomplishes—what a trained mind with a large brain can do—and I feel perfectly hopeless," Alexander confessed to Martha.[16]

FOSSIL HUNTING

Yet, if Alexander never indicated an interest in pursuing a degree in paleontology, she was eager to contribute to the university's research on early life forms. At first, she limited her involvement to funding several of Merriam's fossil hunting expeditions. Then in 1901, Annie decided she wanted to significantly expand her role in the school's paleontological research program by organizing a collecting expedition of her own. When she approached Merriam with her plan, he recommended a site in an old lake bed in the Fossil Lake region of southern Oregon. Relatively young from a geologic perspective, the site was known to be a rich source for the fossils of prehistoric mammals such as woolly mammoths and giant ground sloths. If Alexander would finance the Fossil Lake expedition and contribute all the specimens that she found to the university, Merriam said, he would gladly furnish her with experienced field assistants and logistic guidance.

With the assistance of Merriam's staff, Alexander compiled a list of necessary equipment and supplies for her expedition, including a small stove, a shotgun for hunting rabbits, ducks, and other game for meat, canvas tents, and a sturdy wagon for hauling specimens back to camp from the field. The collecting party would consist of four people: Annie, two of Merriam's male assistants, and Alexander's friend Mary Wilson, a teacher. Annie invited Wilson only after Merriam insisted that it would be improper for her to travel and camp out alone with men. Alexander would have preferred to bring her friend Martha Beckwith, but Martha had long since returned East to pursue her teaching career.

Alexander's party arrived at the Fossil Lake site in late June. Digging the petrified remains out of the lake bed's densely compacted soil was arduous work. Nonetheless, Annie was enraptured by every aspect of fossil collection. "The fever for amassing these strange treasures might make of me a collector of the most greedy type, unmoved by 'threats of Hell or hopes of Paradise,'" she wrote cheerfully to Martha.[17] Alexander was also delighted to be camping out in the wilds again, although she complained to Beckwith that life at the Fossil Lake campsite with its tents, folding cots, and ample supply of canned foods was a bit too civilized for her tastes:

> Once in a while I have a wild desire to strap a roll of blankets on my back with two or three loaves of bread and alone make for some region where the firs grow thick and the streams flow from under banks of snow, leaving my party to shift for themselves.[18]

Alexander was reluctant to see her first collecting expedition end. The trip, she claimed, had afforded her "more amusement" than anything else she had ever done.[19] Nonetheless, she was anxious to have Merriam evaluate the specimens that she and her party had gathered, which comprised over 100 fossils from a variety of extinct mammals, including miniature horses and camels.

SHASTASAURUS AND *THALATTOSAURUS ALEXANDRAE*

After returning from Fossil Lake, Alexander audited another paleontology class and a geology course. "I have not missed a single lecture," she wrote to Martha. Annie continued:

> I like it more and more, this study of our old, old world and the creatures to whom it belonged in the ages past, just as much as it does to us today. Perhaps the study is all the more interesting because it is incomplete, there is so much yet to find out [20]

Her parents did "not seem to quite approve my new ambition," Annie admitted to Beckwith. Nonetheless, Annie was determined to keep on doing what she loved best: "I do not want to be selfish yet it seems to me we have the right to a considerable extent of disposing of our lives as we think fit," she declared to her friend.[21]

The following summer, Alexander financed and organized a second fossil collecting expedition under the tutelage of John Merriam. At his suggestion, she invited a University of California geologist and a Stanford University paleontologist to participate in the trip. Also included in the party was Katherine Jones, a student at Berkeley who was to serve as Annie's requisite female companion. This time Alexander's collecting site was to be in Shasta County in northern California, where Merriam wanted the group to hunt for specimens of the prehistoric marine vertebrate, the ichthyosaur. Ichthyosaurs first evolved from land-dwelling reptiles more than 200 million years ago. Ranging in size from approximately 2 to more than 50 feet in length, they breathed air like all reptiles, yet were fishlike in both movement and appearance.

For an entire month, Alexander's party combed the limestone strata of Shasta County for ichthyosaur remains. Since the fossils were deeply embedded in rock, recovering them was a slow and laborious process. Nonetheless, Alexander was delighted with the expedition, and little wonder: on this, her second collecting trip, she displayed a truly remarkable talent for locating significant fossil material. Undoubtedly, Annie's success had a great deal to do with her willingness, as she put it, to "push through thick brush to the most obscure places with the hope that for that reason they may not have been already visited."[22]

Annie managed to uncover three important ichthyosaur skeletons on the 1902 expedition, including one nearly complete and exceptionally well-preserved specimen. After examining the skeleton, Merriam concluded that it was a new species of ichthyosaur, which he named *Shastasaurus alexandrae* in Annie's honor. (A species is a group of related animals or plants that breed only with others in their group.) Dr. Merriam, Alexander proudly informed Martha, "respects me thoroughly."[23]

The following summer Annie sponsored a second collecting expedition to Shasta County. This time the mandatory second female was Edna Wemple, a paleontology student at Berkeley who would become one of Annie's closest friends. Once again, Alexander demonstrated an almost uncanny knack for uncovering important specimens. Within days of arriving at the new site in Shasta County's black limestone region, Annie had already made the find of the entire expedition: a fossil that Merriam would later identify as a new genus of ichthyosaur and dub *Thalattosaurus alexandrae* as a tribute to his plucky and resourceful benefactress.

SAFARI TO THE "DARK CONTINENT"

Unlike the previous three years, in 1904 Annie did not organize an expedition to collect fossils for John Merriam. Instead, she took part in a different sort of adventure with her father. Early that year, Samuel Alexander, an avid hunter, invited his spirited 36-year-old daughter to join him on a safari to the wilds of eastern Africa. Annie jumped at the chance to spend six months stalking and shooting big game with her favorite traveling companion in what was then known as the "dark continent." "[T]he opportunity," she wrote ecstatically to Martha, "is one of a lifetime."[24]

From the perspective of the early twenty-first century, the Alexanders' safari looks more like a wanton slaughter of innocent and endangered wildlife than the grand adventure that Annie believed it to be. When Annie and her father set off on their expedition 100 years ago, however, the African countryside was teeming with animals. Trophy hunting, it was widely assumed, would have scant impact on the continent's extraordinarily abundant wildlife. Moreover, sport hunting was a cherished tradition in nineteenth- and early twentieth-century North

On her first camping trip to Crater Lake, seen in this photograph, Annie Alexander discovered her life's passion: nature and natural history. Though she never pursued a degree in paleontology, she had a knack for unearthing significant fossils. On only her second expedition, she discovered a new species of ichthyosaur, named *Shastasaurus alexandrae*.

America and Europe, and on both continents, a big game safari in Africa was considered as the ultimate hunting experience for those fortunate few who could afford such costly recreation.

Although it was certainly unusual for a woman to go on safari to Africa in the early 1900s, it was not unheard of, by any means. When Theodore Roosevelt went on his famous safari to East Africa in 1909 shortly after leaving the White House, the former president's hunting companions included the wife and grown daughter of a British acquaintance, Lord Alfred Pease. A year before the Alexanders' safari, the wealthy American businessman William McMillan went big game hunting in Africa with his wife Lucy, who enjoyed the experience so much she accompanied her husband on another safari in 1905. That same year, Delia Denning Akeley traveled to East Africa with her husband Carl to hunt and collect zoological specimens for the Field Museum of Chicago. Among other trophies, Delia bagged two elephants. The list goes on: in 1910, for example, the American millionaire Kenyon Painter brought his new bride, Maud Wyeth Painter, to East Africa on an exotic "honeymoon safari" that would prove to be the first in a series of African hunting expeditions the couple took together.[25] Like Annie Alexander, these intrepid female hunters of the early twentieth century were every bit as captivated by the mystique and danger of a safari to the dark continent as were their male companions.

THE LUNATIC EXPRESS

In April 1904, Samuel and Annie sailed to Europe and from there to the port of Mombasa in British East Africa, which is present-day Kenya, by way of the Mediterranean Sea and the Suez Canal. From Mombasa, the Alexanders were to journey by train to the city of Nairobi, 250 miles to the northwest. There, Samuel planned to hire native porters and guides to accompany him and Annie on what he envisioned as an 800-mile-long trek through the interior of British East Africa, an area widely considered as the best hunting ground in all of Africa.

The railway that linked Mombasa to Nairobi and then continued northwestward to Port Florence on the big inland sea, Lake Victoria was popularly known as the "Lunatic Express." Attempting to construct a railroad across the lion-infested jungles, rugged mountain ranges, and vast deserts of British East Africa's unsettled interior was insane, many people said, when the project was begun in the mid-1890s. Indeed, the "Lunatic Express" would more than live up to its nickname. Completed just a year before the Alexanders arrived in British East Africa, the Express took nearly a decade to finish and cost twice as much to build as was originally estimated. Tragically, dozens of the natives hired to lay the railroad's hundreds of miles of track died during its construction. Although most of the fallen workers succumbed to malaria, dysentery, or heat stroke, a horrifying number were devoured by lions.

Since the British authorities had established a game reserve extending for several miles north and south of the tracks, Annie was able to glimpse vast herds of exotic creatures from the window of her railway car on the 12-hour trip to Nairobi, animals that few of her compatriots had ever even heard of, much less seen. To Annie's delight, now and then a stray gazelle or zebra would wander right up to the edge of the tracks, venturing so close to her railway car that she could almost touch them.

THE THRILL OF THE CHASE

At Nairobi, Samuel and Annie bade farewell to the Lunatic Express and set about the task of locating porters and guides to assist them on their long journey across British East Africa. Each of the nearly 70 porters they hired would be responsible for carrying up to 65 pounds of supplies and equipment on his head (the maximum weight allowed by law). Among the items that the men would be expected to haul were guns, boxes of ammunition, tents, bandages and other medical supplies, cooking utensils, foodstuffs, an ample stock of blankets (because even in Africa, nights can be chilly at higher elevations), and three big cameras. These last items belonged to Annie, who was determined to bring plenty of photographs of the African landscape home with her along with her hunting trophies.

When all of the arrangements had finally been made, the Alexanders and their large entourage boarded a train for Nakuru, a six-hour journey north of Nairobi. At nearby Lake Naaivasha, Annie and Samuel established their first camp. Over the course of the next several months, they would trek slowly northward to Lake Baringo, then westward as far as Port Florence, and finally northward again to the vicinity of Mount Elgon, shooting game and photographs all along the way.

On their safari, Annie and Samuel did not merely hunt for sport. As expedition leaders, they were expected to furnish their numerous porters and guides with a daily supply of fresh meat. Annie, who had presumably learned to shoot from her father, did more than her part in meeting the daily meat quota. Annie "has developed into a very fine shot," Samuel noted proudly in a letter to his wife. "She can put a ball through an animal's neck at 100 yards most every time. In fact, on this trip, she has brought from 200 to 400 pounds of meat into camp most every day." [26]

Annie and Samuel hunted gazelles, impalas, zebras, water-bucks, hartebeests, and ostriches with notable success for meat

THE ALEXANDERS GO ELEPHANT HUNTING

Shortly before the end of their safari, while visiting acquaintances in Kijabe, British East Africa, the Alexanders went elephant hunting with a "Mr. Stauffacher," a local missionary. Stauffacher led Annie and Samuel into a dense forest where the trio soon spotted fresh elephant tracks. Minutes later, nine or ten elephants were charging straight at them. There was no trumpeting, only the sound of cracking boughs as the huge animals crashed through the jungle. Terrified, Annie and Samuel ducked behind a nearby tree. Inexplicably, the herd suddenly divided with several of the elephants veering off one way and the rest another. Annie and Samuel quickly raised their guns and took aim. A huge male with tusks more than four feet long crashed to the ground, mortally wounded. Later that day, the Alexanders posed proudly for a photograph sitting atop their "trophy."

Hunting elephants for sport has been prohibited since 1977 in the former nation of British East Africa, which is and for trophies. Although she stalked and killed her prey with no apparent remorse, Annie prided herself on being a naturalist as well as a hunter and routinely noted the behavior and physical characteristics of the animals she pursued. Two creatures that Alexander shrank from hunting were monkeys and giraffes. To shoot monkeys, Annie wrote to her mother, would seem "more like murder" than sport.[27] The lofty giraffes, she felt, "with their heads 20 feet in the air, walking in Indian file like so many ships of the forest," were too graceful and beautiful to kill.[28]

One widely sought-after big game trophy that eluded Annie and her father was the lion. Samuel, however, was confident that if they ever chanced to encounter one of those mighty

now Kenya. During the 1980s, however, ivory-hungry poachers quickly replaced trophy seekers as the greatest threat to Kenya's elephant population. By 1989, an estimated 16,000 elephants were left in the country, down from perhaps 125,000 just 20 years earlier. That same year an international conference on endangered species finally outlawed the ivory trade, virtually eliminating elephant poaching throughout Africa.

Since 1989, Kenya's elephant population has doubled. At the same time, however, its human population has swelled by nearly 10 million. Now the biggest threat to Kenya's elephants are conflicts with the growing numbers of humans with whom they must share the country and particularly with farmers, who complain that the animals trample and devour their crops. In an effort to bring the booming elephant population under control, an innovative elephant birth control program was recently instituted in Kenya in which a portion of the adult female population is injected with a contraceptive vaccine.

predators, Annie would prove up to the challenge. In a letter to his son, Annie's younger brother, Wallace, he wrote:

> An Austrian Count returned about two weeks ago from a shooting trip with *nine* lion skins. He came, however, in one case, very near being killed. If it had not been for his brave gun carrier, who brained the lion when it was on top of him, he would have been killed. I have the *same gun bearer*, and if he cannot handle the lion I know that Annie will sieze [*sic*] it by the tail and sling it 20 feet away.[29]

Samuel also had no concerns regarding his daughter's ability to withstand the arduous physical demands of hiking hundreds of miles across rugged terrain, often beneath a searing sun. A few weeks into the expedition, he assured his wife that Annie was holding up splendidly: "Annie seems to flourish in this heat. She has a fine appetite, sleeps well, and can stand any amount of tramping."[30] Annie, he remarked admiringly in another letter home, "is made of good stuff."[31] Although people who did not know her well often assumed that Annie was delicate because of her small stature and slender build, she actually possessed great physical strength and stamina and would remain remarkably active until well into old age.

TRAGEDY AT VICTORIA FALLS

In late August, with the long safari finally ending, Annie wrote glowingly of her African adventure:

> [T]his trip closes a great chapter. We didn't kill our lion . . . but we saw several large herds of giraffe, and a wild people who went about dressed in skins and hunted with bows and arrows and spears. And we saw every morning the sun rise over miles of tall grass laden with dew . . . and set behind Mt. Elgon whose gradual slopes reminded us very much of Haleakala [32]

A few days later she remarked exultantly in a letter to her mother, "We have made every day count. I doubt if there are two more delighted people in this country than Papa and I."[33]

Before departing Africa to return home, Annie and Samuel decided to travel south to the Zambezi River in what was then the country of Rhodesia to view the celebrated Victoria Falls. Considered one of the seven natural wonders of the world, the huge waterfalls are one mile wide and plunge some 350 feet.

For two days, the Alexanders admired the immense curtain of water from a number of different vantage points, with Annie taking plenty of photographs. On September 9, their third day at Victoria Falls, Annie and Samuel descended a steep ravine to the edge of the Zambezi River so that Annie could take pictures of the waterfalls at their exit site. High above the pair, workers were busily digging out the foundation for what would be the famed Zambezi Railway Bridge. Completed in 1905, the bridge spans the gorge through which the Zambezi River flows just beneath the falls, linking the modern-day nations of Zambia and Zimbabwe (formerly Northern and Southern Rhodesia).

Now and then, small rocks and clods of dirt would fall down the steep slope from the spot where the workers were excavating. Samuel and Annie, however, stayed put, never imagining that they were in any real danger. Suddenly, a large boulder hurtled down the ravine toward the Alexanders. The rock struck Samuel squarely on his left side, smashing his foot and leaving him bleeding profusely. By the time that medical assistance could arrive, Samuel had already lost a dangerous amount of blood. Early the next morning, with Annie by his side, Samuel Alexander breathed his last. After arranging for her father to be buried in the town of Livingston, a few miles away from the falls, Annie embarked on the long and lonely journey back home to California.

5

Alaskan Explorer and Museum Founder

Annie Alexander was devastated by the loss of her beloved parent. On the one-month anniversary of Samuel's death, she wrote to Martha and Mary Beckwith from Oakland:

> I have felt so terribly alone. It is a month today since my darling father died and was buried. It doesn't seem as if I could ever make it seem true. He was so much alive. I knew him so well—every curve in his face and every tone in his voice. It was very, very dreadful to believe.[34]

Seeking a respite from her grief, Annie turned to the paleontological fieldwork that had so enthralled her since her first collecting trip in 1901: "It is strange how absorbing this work is. We forget the outside world," Annie once declared of fossil hunting.[35] With John Merriam's help, she determinedly organized a new paleontological expedition to the limestone hills of northern Nevada for the spring and summer of 1905.

EXPEDITION TO HUMBOLDT RANGE

In May 1905, Alexander, her friend Edna Wemple, several of Dr. Merriam's assistants at Berkeley, and a paleontology professor from Stanford University headed for American Canyon in the West Humboldt Range to search for ichthyosaur remains. Merriam also joined the expedition for a few weeks. According to an account of the trip Annie wrote after returning home to Oakland, the men did most of the heavy digging while she and Edna Wemple "sat in the dust and sun, marking and wrapping bones. No sooner were these loaded in the wagon . . . than new piles took their place."[36] Even though Alexander had financed the expedition, she and Edna assumed the tedious jobs of gathering the firewood and cooking for the rest of the party:

> Night after night we stood before a hot fire to stir rice, or beans, or corn, or soup, contriving the best dinners we

could out of our dwindling supply of provisions," Annie wrote. "We sometimes wondered if the men thought the firewood dropped out of the sky or whether a fairy godmother brought it to our door, for they never asked any questions [37]

Yet, if Annie was often irritated with her unappreciative male companions, she adored being out in the wilds again. Alexander was enchanted by the landscape. She wrote:

Sometimes half a dozen distinct thundershowers would gather and sweep across the valley . . . below us. There was a perpetual scurry of clouds from the northwest. They left their snow on the higher elevations that looked truly Alpine as the sun touched them. . . . All this we witnessed while keeping an eye open for bone, taking in large draughts of bracing air, our warm jersey[s] buttoned up to our necks.[38]

Whenever the weather permitted, Annie slept outside beneath the stars, an experience she always found magical:

People naturally count it among their blessings to have a roof over their heads at night, but how oppressive that roof seems to you, and the four walls of your room after a month or two in the open! Half the universe shone down upon us those clear nights in Nevada; not a tree to break the wonderful arch of the Milky Way reaching from horizon to horizon. The same constellations seen night after night as we lay on our backs on the ground made their impress on our minds that a casual view of them from a bedroom window or city street could never make.[39]

The two-month-long collecting trip was extraordinarily successful. Alexander's party recovered nearly 30 specimens of ichthyosaur from the limestone embankments of the West Humboldt Range, including the single most complete ichthyosaur skeleton ever to be discovered in North America. One of the skeletons that they retrieved "was of truly lordly proportions . . . For two days I watched with fascinated eyes the work of excavation . . .The specimen was measured and found to be 25 feet long," Alexander wrote. [40] Later, Alexander mused:

> Think what countless and diverse races have walked or crawled or swum on the earth and become extinct since that remote time! . . . It is a thrilling thought to the fossil hunter that he is privileged to reach back in the world's history and uncover some of its ancient pages.[41]

AMERICA'S "LAST FRONTIER"

Despite the success of her fossil collecting expedition to Nevada, however, Annie was eager to try a new sort of adventure the following summer. For some time, she had been toying with the idea of traveling to what was then popularly known as America's "last frontier": Alaska.

Within three decades of its purchase from Russia by the United States in 1867, Alaska had already developed a flourishing tourist industry centered on the Inside Passage, the picturesque network of channels and fjords situated between the Canadian coast and the Pacific Ocean. Hordes of American tourists flocked to the new territory by steamship to view the passage's spectacular scenery. While enjoying deluxe accommodations on board, the pampered travelers marveled at immense ice fields, towering glaciers, and lushly forested mountains as their ship glided slowly along Alaska's southern coastline.

A luxurious and restful cruise, however, was not at all the sort of Alaskan adventure that Alexander had in mind. She longed to experience the unspoiled Alaskan wilderness firsthand, not from the distant deck of a steamer. She intended to work hard on her Alaskan excursion, devoting her days to searching out and gathering specimens of the remote territory's abundant wildlife to bring back home to California with her. By 1905, Alexander's scientific interests had expanded to include recent animals as well as extinct ones. Shortly before her trip to Africa, she had begun a collection of the skulls of wild animals. "I have about 45 now representing 40 different species, mostly carnivores. Really you don't know how fascinating it is," she wrote enthusiastically to Martha regarding her new avocation.[42]

In late 1905, a meeting with C. Hart Merriam, the chief of the United States Biological Survey in Washington, D.C., served to deepen Alexander's burgeoning interest in both zoology and Alaska. While visiting his cousin, John Merriam in Berkeley, on John's suggestion, Hart traveled to Oakland to examine Annie's skull collection, which included a number of rare specimens that she had obtained in British East Africa the previous year. After viewing her collection, Hart spoke at length with Alexander about Alaska, which he had visited in 1899 as part of the highly publicized Harriman Expedition. Organized by railroad tycoon E. H. Harriman, the two-month-long, 126-member research expedition included hunters, photographers, and scientists, and collected hundreds of specimens of mammals, birds, insects, and plants from Alaska's coastal regions. Over the few years following Harriman's excursion, several smaller United States–sponsored research expeditions had also scoured Alaska's coastline for samples of its fauna and flora. (Fauna and flora are the animals and plants of a given era or locale considered as a whole.) Nonetheless, in 1905, when Annie was contemplating her expedition, United

States scientists still had little knowledge of the plant and animal life of much of the interior of the mainland or of the densely forested and mostly uninhabited islands that dotted Alaska's shores.

STALKING THE ELUSIVE GRIZZLY

After talking with C. Hart Merriam regarding his adventures in the northern territory, Alexander was more determined than ever to see America's "last frontier" for herself. She also resolved to bring back specimens of Alaskan bears for Hart, whose chief area of research was the "taxonomy" (or scientific classification) of North American bears. On Merriam's recommendation, Alexander invited Alvin Seale, a government-appointed wildlife collector, to accompany her. Annie paid Seale's salary during the duration of the trip and provided all the necessary camping gear and other supplies and equipment for the expedition. Needing a female companion, Alexander also asked her good friend Edna Wemple to go along.

Alexander, Wemple, and Seale arrived in Juneau, Alaska in May 1906. From Juneau they traveled westward by boat to the Kenai Peninsula in south-central Alaska, an area largely ignored by previous scientific expeditions. Hiking inland to Skilak Lake, Alexander's party set up camp and began hunting and trapping a variety of birds and small mammals, including porcupines, sea otters, minks, and ermines. Annie was entranced by the sight of grizzly bears (or brown bears as they are more often called today) lumbering along the hillsides. To her disappointment, however, the animals stayed well out of rifle range.

In September, Alexander's expedition departed the Kenai Peninsula for nearby Kodiak Island, famed for its abundant bear population. On Kodiak, the party collected more bird and mammal specimens but still could not secure a grizzly. Before returning home, however, Alexander bought an enormous brown bear from a local trapper. C. Hart Merriam would later identify the specimen as a new subspecies of grizzly bear, naming it *Ursus alexandrae* in Annie's honor.

In October, after four months in the Alaskan wilderness, Alexander and her little group finally headed back to California. Despite bloodthirsty mosquitoes, frequent rain, and the difficulties of slogging through deep mud, and occasionally snow, in heavy rubber boots, Annie was enraptured by her first experience with the northern territory and its verdant rainforests, snow-capped mountains, and bountiful wildlife. Almost immediately, she began making plans for a second Alaskan expedition.

THE ALEXANDER ARCHIPELAGO

For her second foray into Alaska in the summer of 1907, Annie decided to visit the Alexander Archipelago (named for the Russian czar, Alexander), a chain of islands off the territory's southeastern coast. As of 1907, no scientific party had ever visited the interiors of these heavily forested and mountainous islands.

This time around, Alexander's group consisted of mammalogist Frank Stephens and his wife Kate, a malacologist (a scientist who studies mollusks such as snails and squid), and two male wildlife collectors recommended by C. Hart Merriam. Mrs. Stephens would take Edna Wemple's place as the requisite second female. Edna had recently married and although she would remain one of Alexander's closest friends for the rest of her life, she would never again accompany Annie on a scientific expedition.

The Alexander Archipelago consists of some 1,000 small islands, but Annie and her group planned to concentrate their attention on just three islands in the northern part of the chain that C. Hart Merriam believed to contain large bear populations: Admiralty, Baranof, and Chichagof. The group sailed first to Admiralty, the closest of the three islands to the mainland.

Alexander's party pitched six tents on Admiralty's east shore: three for sleeping, one for storing supplies, one for cooking, and the last for "putting up" specimens. Putting up specimens was a time consuming process that entailed carefully skinning the animals that had been trapped or shot by the party, filling the pelts with wire and cotton, and pinning them to a strip of wood to dry. Along with their skins, the animals' skeletons were also saved. All soft tissue, including muscle and internal organs, however, was usually thrown out, and peeling away every bit of tissue clinging to the bones was a painstaking and slow task.

Perhaps the most challenging specimens to put up were birds. Especially delicate and thin, bird skins are easily torn or stretched out of shape. On her second Alaskan expedition, Annie devoted many of her evenings to learning "how to put up a good bird skin—one can master the mechanical part with a little practice, but the real art lies in the finishing touches, shaping the specimen and making the feathers lie right."[43]

After several weeks, Alexander decided to push farther inland in search of bears for C. Hart Merriam's research. Although her party never managed to locate the elusive bears, they discovered a plentiful population of beavers living in Admiralty's densely forested interior, marking the first time these mammals had ever been reported on any of the islands of southeastern Alaska. They also explored a series of small lakes previously unknown to mapmakers. Alexander's companions insisted on dubbing one of them Alexander Lake in honor of their expedition's generous and energetic leader.

From Admiralty Island, the group sailed west and north to Baranof and Chichagof Islands, finally ending up at the Beardslee Islands near the entrance to Glacier Bay. On the Fourth of July, the temperature actually climbed to 60 degrees Fahrenheit and the party decided to make ice cream from canned condensed milk mixed with pieces of an iceberg that they had found floating in the frigid waters near their campsite.

Although Annie's attempts at bear hunting once again proved unsuccessful, when her party returned home at the end of the summer, they carried with them 476 mammal specimens and 532 bird skins, including several animals later determined to be new species, and more than 30 sets of eggs.

PRINCE WILLIAM SOUND AND "A DANDY GIRL"

In 1908, Annie decided to undertake one last scientific expedition to the far north. This time her collecting locale was to be Prince William Sound in south-central Alaska. Annie was intrigued by reports of this beautiful and virtually unexplored wilderness surrounded by soaring mountains and dotted with dozens of small, lushly forested islands.

On her third Alaskan expedition, Annie was again accompanied by two male collectors recommended to her by C. Hart Merriam. Since Kate and Frank Stephens declined to participate in this trip, Annie was left with the problem of locating a suitable female traveling companion for herself. Her determination to bring another woman along seemed to have been rooted more in her concerns regarding the reputations of her male companions than in any worries she had regarding her own good name. "I've decided to take a lady with me on the Alaska trip if I can find the right one. I don't want my collectors to suffer any unpleasantness from talk on my account," she informed a male acquaintance just one month before the expedition was scheduled to begin.[44]

Finally, at the very last minute, Annie found her mandatory female companion, Louise Kellogg, a neighbor from Oakland. At 28, Kellogg was 13 years younger than Annie. Like Alexander, she was single and still resided with her parents. A schoolteacher, Louise had a degree in literature from the University of California and no previous experience with biological fieldwork. Nonetheless, she was an accomplished outdoorswoman, having been taught to fish and shoot at an early age by her father, an expert hunter and angler.

Adventurous, athletic, and eager to learn everything that she could about zoological collecting, Kellogg was "a dandy girl," and Alexander was convinced she was sure to make an outstanding addition to the scientific party.[45]

In May 1907, Alexander, Kellogg, and the rest of the small group arrived at Hinchinbrook Island in the Prince William Sound. From there, spending about a week at each site, they "island hopped" in an effort to sample the wildlife of the entire area. Mornings were typically devoted to hunting birds or inspecting trap lines in the field with afternoons and evenings usually spent in camp, putting up specimens.

In September, the group departed Prince William Sound with an assortment of bird and mammal specimens and an eight-foot-tall male brown bear that a local hunter had trapped for them on Montague Island, one of the last islands they visited. Louise had turned out to be as competent a field naturalist and camper as Alexander had hoped she would be. As Edmund Heller, one of the collectors on the expedition declared of the spunky schoolteacher, "Miss Kellogg . . . is the right sort, without any yellow streak or quitting propensities."[46] The "greatest discovery of this trip," Annie informed Martha, "was Louise."[47]

FOUNDING A NATURAL HISTORY MUSEUM

Ever since the terrible accident that had claimed Samuel Alexander's life in 1904, his grieving daughter had been searching for "something to do to divert my mind and absorb my interest," as Annie would write many years later.[48] The sudden death of her cherished parent had made Alexander more anxious than ever to find "a life work," an endeavor in which she could effectively invest her considerable talents, energy, and financial resources.[49]

Like her hard-working missionary grandparents and farmer-entrepreneur father before her, Annie felt compelled to make every minute of her time on earth count, achieving something of lasting value before her death. Although she found her annual field trips into the wilderness deeply satisfying, merely collecting zoological or fossil specimens was not enough for Alexander. By 1907, she had determined what her "life work" was to be: she would found a natural history museum, a research institution whose chief focus would be the wildlife with which she was most familiar: the fauna of the American West. Almost immediately, she resolved to build her new research facility at the University of California at Berkeley, the one institution of higher learning with which she had established close ties over the years.

When Annie shared her plan to found a museum devoted to western fauna with her friend, C. Hart Merriam, the survey chief encouraged Alexander to launch her project as soon as possible. As more and more of the West succumbed to urban and agricultural development, the area's once abundant animal life was disappearing at an alarming rate, Hart declared. In the fastest growing part of the West, Annie's home state of California, the problem was particularly acute. Since 1850, the state's population had mushroomed from 90,000 to over 2 million. California's burgeoning population combined with rapid agricultural expansion was destroying the natural habitats of an ever-rising portion of the state's birds and mammals as forests were cut down and more and more land was farmed or fenced in for livestock. Even as early as 1907, several indigenous species, including the brown bear, the California valley antelope, and the California white-tail deer had already vanished from the state in the wake of habitat destruction and over-hunting, while many other species such as the beaver were becoming scarce. Extensive samples of native animals needed to be gathered, described, and preserved as soon as possible, C. Hart Merriam argued, if an accurate and comprehensive account of the vertebrate fauna of California and the rest of the western United States was to be compiled for future generations.

The early nineteenth century saw an explosion of urban and agricultural development in the West, which threatened plant and animal species in the area. This problem was especially severe in Annie's home state of California. Her work in developing the University of California's Museum of Vertebrate Zoology was essential in encouraging research to potentially save much of the nation's endangered wildlife.

In addition to creating a museum that would describe, classify, and preserve samples of the West's still existing verte-brate fauna for posterity, Annie wanted to establish an institution whose collections would enhance the scientific community's understanding of "the important biological issues of the day," and particularly the theories of natural selection and evolution developed by the great nineteenth-century English biologist, Charles Darwin.[50] Annie realized that both zoologists and paleontologists depended on preserved specimens of recent animals in their efforts to understand such complex evolutionary problems as how new species originate or how rapidly they evolve over time. Indeed, Annie's onetime paleontology professor, John C. Merriam, strongly supported her efforts to establish a zoological research museum at Berkeley, noting that although he routinely needed to compare fossil specimens with their modern-day ancestors, all the major collections of recent vertebrates were located many miles away in the Midwest or on the East Coast. An extensive collection of zoological specimen materials on the West Coast would significantly boost his research abilities and those of other paleontologists at the university as well, Merriam declared.

JOSEPH GRINNELL

In 1907, as Annie was formulating her plans for a zoological museum at the University of California, she met a young man who was destined to play a vital role in the future of her research facility. His name was Joseph Grinnell and he was a biology teacher at the Throop Polytechnic Institute in Pasadena (later the California Institute of Technology) and an acquaintance of C. Hart Merriam. When he was not teaching, Grinnell devoted as much of his time as possible to fieldwork, collecting zoological specimens in California, Alaska, and throughout the American West. Annie was deeply impressed by Joseph's obvious devotion to biological fieldwork and research, especially after viewing the miniature natural history museum he had created in his home's back parlor with its thousands of meticulously prepared and arranged specimens. Alexander particularly admired Grinnell's extensive field notes, which he supplemented with numerous photographs and detailed maps of the specimens' natural habits.

After discussing her museum project with Grinnell, Annie became convinced that Joseph not only possessed the experience, dedication, and skills necessary to administer her new

Annie Montague
Alexander in
Her Own Words

From Annie Montague Alexander's Accounts

Annie Montague Alexander provided the funds for a paleontological expedition that yielded more than two dozen ichthyosaur specimens under the leadership of John Merriam. Alexander, who was also a member of the team, recorded an account of the trip to the West Humboldt Range in Nevada in 1905. The following excerpts are from that account:

"The resurrection call aroused another Saurian [ichthyosaur] from his long sleep. After a course in purgatory in which he will be divested of his limestone encasement he ought to shine as one of the foremost lights in the new museum at Berkeley, for he was a saurian of truly lordly proportions . . . For two days I watched with fascinated eyes the work of excavation . . . The specimen was measured and founded to be twenty-five feet long."[i]

"People naturally count it among their blessings to have a roof over their heads at night, but how oppressive that roof seems to you, and the four walls of your room after a month or two in the open! Half the universe shone down upon us those clear nights in Nevada; not a tree to break the wonderful arch of the Milky Way reaching from horizon to horizon. The same constellations seen night after night as we lay on our backs on the ground made their impress on our minds that a casual view of them from a bedroom window or city street could never make."[ii]

"We worked hard up to the last. My dear friend Miss Wemple stood by me through thick and thin. Together we sat in the dust and sun, marking and wrapping bones. No sooner were these loaded in the wagon . . . than new piles took their places. Night after night we stood before a hot fire to stir rice, or beans, or corn, or soup, contriving the best dinners we could out of our dwindling supply of provisions. We sometimes wondered if the men thought the fire wood dropped out of the sky or whether a fairy godmother brought it to our door, for they never asked any questions."[iii]

Writing to her friend Martha Beckwith in 1922, Alexander describes a paleontological field trip to California's Mojave Desert that she took with Louise Kellogg:

"We have been such busy mortals! Wouldn't you think you were busy if you had been working for a half a month with pick and shovel digging a camel out of the ground? More than that we have been on our knees with jackknife and chisel following the bone along with a caution and patience I didn't know we possessed. The excitement of the chase never quite equaled this. First we found the forelimbs with vertebrate, limbs, and small bones mixed up with it. Then six neck vertebrae beginning with the atlas and axis. These half then encircled the skull, the greatest prize of all and in front of this the lower jaw complete and the scapula with more vertebrae and ribs. . . . [T]he camel isn't our only specimen I can boastfully say. We never go out looking but what we find something. Just this morning Louise picked up part of a horse jaw and a good deer jaw with teeth, the little *Merycodus*, in places we have crossed several times so a fossil hunter's work is never finished . . . . It is strange how absorbing this work is. We forget the outside world."[ix]

i. Quoted in *http://www.ucmp.berkeley.edu/archives/saurian.html*.

ii. Quoted in Stein, *On Her Own Terms*, p. 51.

iii. Quoted in *http://www.ucmp.berkeley.edu/history/alexander.html*.

ix. Quoted in Stein, *On Her Own Terms*, p. 188.

Haleakala

Mount Haleakala was a constant part of Annie Alexander's childhood, dominating the landscape of her native Maui. Haleakala is a dormant volcano, rising more than 10,000 feet above sea level and 30,000 feet below. The mountain is composed of thick hardened lava, though its crater is a result of years of erosion rather than volcanic activity.

....

Silversword

Silversword is one of several plant and animal species that inhabit Mount Haleakala. This silver-leafed plant was abundant on the volcano's crater floor until its existence was threatened by tourists and grazing animals in the mid-twentieth century. Fortunately, Mount Haleakala was declared a national park in 1961, and with the help of conservationists, silversword has begun to flourish again.

John Merriam

John Merriam's paleontology lectures at the University of California immediately inspired Alexander to explore natural history. Merriam was a popular and respected professor and researcher of early life forms, and his support and tutelage encouraged Alexander to first fund University fossil hunts and then embark on her own digs.

Saurian Expedition

One of Alexander's digs with Dr. Merriam took her to the Humboldt Range in Nevada to explore the limestones in the region and search for ichthyosaur remains. The trip was extremely successful, with the group finding over two dozen ichthyosaur specimens, including the most complete fossil of that species ever found in North America. Alexander, dressed for fieldwork in a skirt, stands to the right in this picture.

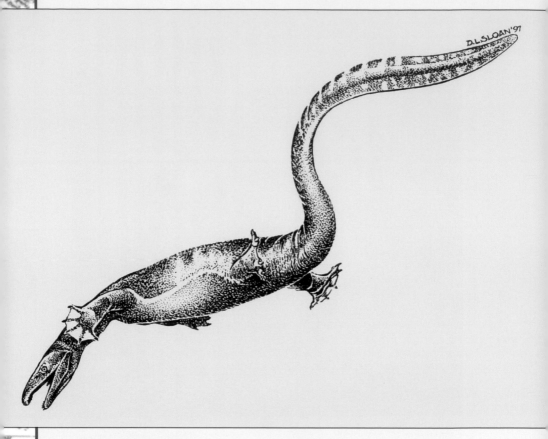

Thallatosaurus

On her second expedition under Dr. Merriam, Alexander traveled to Shasta County in northern California to hunt for ichthyosaurs. Her talent for finding fossils was first evident on this trip, during which Alexander uncovered several important skeletons, including that of a new species named *Shastasaurus alexandrae* in her honor. The next summer, Alexander returned to the area for another expedition, this time discovering a new ichthyosaur genus later called *Thalattosaurus alexandrae*.

facility but also shared her vision regarding the institution's fundamental goals and needs. Like Alexander, Grinnell envisioned the development of a research center at Berkeley that would rival the finest natural history museums in the eastern United States, including the Smithsonian in Washington, D.C., and the Academy of Natural Sciences in Philadelphia. After only a few meetings with the young Pasadena teacher, Alexander was sure that she had found in the determined and hardworking Joseph Grinnell precisely the right person to direct her museum.

A DETERMINED NEGOTIATOR

In October 1907, Alexander was ready to formally approach Benjamin Wheeler, the President of the University of California, with her plan for a museum at Berkeley:

> Should the University of California . . . erect a galvanized iron building furnished with electric light, heat and janitor's services and turn it over to my entire control as a Museum of Natural History for the next seven years, I will guarantee the expenditure of $7000 yearly during that time for field and research work relating exclusively to mammals, birds, and reptiles of the West Coast, with the understanding that the University of California would be in no way responsible for the management of the funds for carrying out the work, or selection of collectors.[51]

According to Alexander's specifications, the museum's collections and research was to concentrate on terrestrial vertebrates (mammals, birds, and reptiles); Alexander excluded marine vertebrates because nearby Stanford University already possessed an extensive collection of fish specimens.

In an era when women were expected to submit to the leadership of men both in the public and private spheres,

Alexander's insistence that she retain absolute control over the museum's financial affairs, field collectors, and program of research in her proposal to Wheeler and the all-male Board of Regents was bold. Moreover, Alexander stipulated that she would not hand over any money for the new facility unless Joseph Grinnell was appointed as its first director. Although the day would come when Grinnell would be considered as one of the country's leading evolutionary biologists, in 1907, Grinnell was an obscure science instructor who had yet to even complete his Ph.D. "I am not so disinterested a giver as the University might like to have me," Annie admitted in a letter to Wheeler after the president took his time about replying to her proposal. "Were I to turn the funds over to the University to control . . . I should feel quite

COLLECTING JERBOAS AND A "PHARAOH'S RAT"

In the winter of 1924, Annie Alexander and Louise Kellogg decided to take an excursion to Egypt. Although the primary purpose of the trip was sightseeing, Alexander could not resist the chance to collect interesting zoological specimens for the Museum of Vertebrate Zoology which, although focused on the fauna of the western United States, also included specimens from other parts of North America and the world.

Before linking up with a touring party in Cairo, Alexander and Kellogg took a weeklong camping trip into the desert accompanied by Egyptian guides. Apparently at Grinnell's request, their main objective was to collect jerboas, a jumping rodent with a long tail and hind legs similar to the kangaroo rats of the American Southwest. The women delighted in riding camels through the desert and watching the sunrise with the Great Pyramid in the foreground. Although Annie set plenty of traps, however, she only caught a few gerbils and no jerboas.

out of it. Some responsibility in the work is necessary to my own well-being and a legitimate incentive to see the enterprise develop," she declared.[52]

Negotiations between Alexander and the University dragged on for months, but in early 1908 Wheeler and the Board of Regents finally agreed to all of Annie's demands regarding the proposed museum, including the appointment of the little known Grinnell as the facility's top adminis-trator. As Barbara Stein points out, Wheeler and the Regents probably hoped that the new zoological research center would bring added attention and prestige to the University of California, which was still young compared to the leading eastern universities and had yet to achieve a national reputation.

> **Back in Cairo, Alexander finally bought a jerboa from an Arab trapper.** The trapper also sold her several snakes and a curious little black-and-white animal that he called a "Pharaoh's Rat" but which looked an awful lot like a skunk. At their hotel, Alexander and Kellogg thoroughly examined the dead specimen and came to the conclusion that their "Pharaoh's Rat" was probably a zorilla, a close relative of the North American skunk. Not to be deterred, the women boldly proceeded to put up the zorilla in their hotel room. "Skinning and the smell were the [proof]," the unflappable Kellogg wrote in her diary, observing matter-of-factly, "It was not as odoriferous as our skunk or we never could have [prepared it] in the hotel."*
>
> * Quoted in Barbara R. Stein, *On Her Own Terms: Annie Montague Alexander and the Rise of Science in the American West*. Berkeley: Univ. of California Press, 2001.

THE MUSEUM OF VERTEBRATE
ZOOLOGY OPENS ITS DOORS

By mid-1908, Annie was able to inform Grinnell that work on the new facility had begun and in January 1909, the Museum of Vertebrate Zoology (MVZ) officially opened its doors on the Berkeley campus. Alexander promptly turned over to the facility her extensive personal collection of some 3,500 mammal and bird specimens to serve as the core of the new museum's holdings.

For the first two years of the MVZ's existence, the facility's main hall was open to the public for several hours each week. There museum visitors could view three large dioramas featuring a variety of West Coast animals that had been preserved, stuffed, and mounted in lifelike poses. Deeply concerned about the West's rapidly declining animal population, Alexander hoped that the exhibits would help to increase public awareness of the western United States' unique fauna and spur interest in conservation and habitat protection. In 1911, however, Annie withdrew her financial support for public exhibits at the MVZ, after concluding that the thousands of dollars it cost her to have the dioramas created would be better spent on the museum's chief mission: scientific research. Moreover, since Alexander was giving the MVZ enough money to support at least one collecting party in the field nearly year-round, the museum's collections were growing rapidly, and the large amount of space required for the public exhibits would soon be needed to store study specimens. Even after abandoning the exhibits, however, Alexander continued her commitment to educating the public regarding wildlife conservation through various museum publications and lecture series aimed at a popular audience.

As Annie had foreseen, Joseph Grinnell was an outstanding director for her museum. Under Grinnell's skillful supervision, the museum quickly became the premier center for the study of vertebrate zoology in the western United States. Within a decade of its founding, the MVZ had already gained national and international recognition for its research programs and scholarly publications, particularly in evolutionary biology and systematic "zoology" (the scientific classification of animals). Delighted by the museum's success, in 1919 Alexander established a generous endowment to fund the MVZ permanently.

6

Fieldwork and Land of Her Own

Annie Montague Alexander's commitment to promoting science at the University of California was not restricted to support of her zoological museum and its research endeavors following the MVZ's creation in 1908. Annie continued to provide generous support to the university's paleontological research program and fought determinedly with school administrators to have a separate paleontology department established at Berkeley in 1908 and 1909. As was the case at many colleges and universities of the era, at the University of California paleontology was included within the geology department. Both Annie and her mentor John Merriam were convinced that paleontological research at Berkeley would be strengthened if the two disciplines were split. In 1910, Annie finally won her two-year-long crusade to separate geology and paleontology at Berkeley when a Department of Paleontology was established with John Merriam as chair.

TAKING UP FARMING
On the expedition to Prince William Sound in 1908, Louise Kellogg had proven herself a skilled and tireless field collector with a genuine appreciation for nature and wilderness living. In 1910, tired of the constant struggle of having to locate a suitable female companion every time that she wanted to conduct fieldwork, Alexander persuaded Kellogg to give up teaching to act as her full-time collecting partner. The following year, the energetic pair embarked on an ambitious new enterprise designed to occupy them when they were not engaged in scientific fieldwork.

In 1911, Alexander and Kellogg purchased 525 acres of land on largely undeveloped Grizzly Island in the Suisan Bay, about 40 miles from Oakland. Although their new property was almost entirely swampland, the women were determined to farm it. After months of hard labor, with Alexander and Kellogg toiling side-by-side with their hired field hands, the land was at last drained, cleared, and ready for plowing.

Given that one of Annie's chief motivations for founding the Museum of Vertebrate Zoology was the swiftness with which California's native fauna was disappearing in the wake of agricultural development, it seems ironic that Alexander would have willingly contributed to the destruction of some of her state's richest wildlife habitats by draining hundreds of acres of marshland. Marshland, as Alexander undoubtedly realized, sustains an abundant array of plants such as cattails and bulrushes that in turn provide food and shelter for a large and diverse population of animals, including swans, ducks, geese, beaver, and river otter, to name a few. Yet, as Barbara Stein points out, it would be unfair to judge Alexander's actions according to current principles and perceptions regarding wetland conservation. (Wetlands, which include marshes and bogs, are lands with a spongy, damp soil.) During the early twentieth century, just about everyone in California took for granted "that the state would be developed, that its population would increase, and that a pristine wilderness would eventually vanish," writes Stein.[53]

Wildlife would have to make way for human progress, most people assumed, and thus in 1911, acre upon acre of meadows, forests, wetland and, owing to government-funded irrigation projects, even deserts, were being converted into farm fields all across the state.

CATTLE AND ASPARAGUS

After a few years of growing hay on their new farm, Alexander and Kellogg decided to switch to raising dairy cattle. In the hope of attracting buyers for their purebred livestock, the women traveled all over California, displaying the animals at local, county, and state fairs. From the start, their cattle won prizes, both from within the cattle breeding industry and from the University of California's animal science department.

To Alexander's dismay, however, raising cattle was a more time-consuming enterprise than she had anticipated. The animals required nearly constant attention, leaving Annie little opportunity to go on collecting trips to the mountains or the desert. "I'm just hungry for the wilds," a restless Alexander complained to Martha Beckwith in 1919.[54] That year, Alexander and Kellogg finally decided to sell their troublesome herd and start growing asparagus, a considerably less demanding type of farming than raising purebred cattle. Since asparagus is harvested in the spring, the partners' summers would now be wide open for collecting trips. Alexander planned to divide her winters between Hawaii, where her younger sister Martha and her husband and children now lived, and field excursions in California and elsewhere in the West. Within a few years of the change from cattle to asparagus, Alexander had hired a neighbor to assume the day-to-day running of the Grizzly Island farm, giving her and Kellogg even more freedom to travel.

A CONTINUING COMMITMENT
TO PALEONTOLOGY

In 1920, Alexander received a serious blow when John Merriam, the chair of the new Department of Paleontology, which she had worked so diligently to create, and the University's foremost paleontologist, left Berkeley for a higher paying administrative position in Washington, D.C. "Dr. Merriam's disaffection and desertion of his Department which has owed much of its development to my support of research work since 1900 . . . has made me in a way lose my sense of direction," she wrote bitterly to Joseph Grinnell.[55]

Alexander was even more incensed when Merriam, who retained a research appointment in the Department of Paleontology, tried to continue directing the department and the ample research funds she was still giving to it from afar. In an effort to circumvent Merriam's ongoing influence within the Museum of Paleontology, the department of paleontology's chief research facility on campus, in 1921 Alexander provided the funds to establish the museum as a completely separate unit at Berkeley. Like the MVZ, the University of California's Museum of Paleontology (UCMP) was to be an independent research institution within the university under Alexander's supervision. In 1934, Alexander set up an endowment fund for the UCMP in order "to safeguard for the future the care of collections on which I have already expended many thousands of dollars," she declared.[56]

COLLECTING FOR THE MVZ

Although her financial commitment to paleontological research at the University of California remained strong during the 1920s and 1930s, in her fieldwork Alexander now concentrated on collecting zoological specimens, particularly small mammals, for the Museum of Vertebrate Zoology. As the standing of Joseph Grinnell and the holdings and research programs of the MVZ continued to grow within the scientific community, Alexander became more determined than ever to make her museum the equal of any natural history museum in the eastern United States.

Typically lasting from between one to six months, Alexander and Kellogg's zoological collecting trips focused almost exclusively on California and other western locales. Since her goal as a collector was not merely to expand the MVZ's holdings but to obtain specimens that related directly to the specific research problems being explored by Grinnell and his staff at the MVZ, Alexander consulted closely with the director in planning her expeditions. In accordance with Grinnell's wishes, Alexander and Kellogg emphasized the trapping of small mammals, including mice, squirrels, prairie dogs, and above all, gophers during most of the 1920s and 1930s. During their free moments in the field, the partners also bird-watched and collected unusual plants for the University herbarium at Berkeley.

In order to obtain the small mammal specimens that Grinnell sought for the MVZ, the women often set out six or seven dozen steel traps a day at their various collecting sites, checking the devices at regular intervals and resetting or moving them as needed. Alexander's drive and dedication as a field collector were legendary. When the specimens that Grinnell had asked Alexander to obtain proved elusive on a field trip to Nevada's Pine Canyon, she and Kellogg set 400 traps a night over a period of several days in a heroic effort to capture their quarry.

In keeping with Grinnell's belief that species must be examined in relation to their environment, Alexander and Kellogg made extensive field observations, carefully noting the terrain and landscape, climatic conditions, plant life, and other aspects of their specimens' natural habitats. Each evening, the pair meticulously transcribed their observations into neatly organized field notebooks, which they would eventually turn over to Grinnell and his staff.

Along with their field journals, the women submitted detailed maps to Grinnell, pinpointing the precise locations where they had collected specimens and numerous photographs of the animals' habitats, in keeping with the exacting protocol that the MVZ director expected all of his field collectors to follow. Although neither woman held an advanced degree in science, Annie and Louise were as thorough in their field research as any of Grinnell's scientists or graduate students at the University of California, sometimes even salvaging the contents of their specimens' stomachs or cheek pouches to send to the MVZ with their other field materials.

Alexander and Kellogg's skillfully prepared study specimens, as well as their meticulous field observations, won the admiration of Grinnell and the MVZ staff. To make accurate and detailed comparisons of size, color patterns, and structural variation, researchers need "study skins" that are as uniform in position and shape as possible. Alexander and Kellogg's study skins displayed excellent uniformity, enhancing their research value for the numerous scientists from all over California and the nation who consulted the MVZ's collections. Moreover,

LAST CHANCE CANYON

Although Alexander and Kellogg had already begun to concentrate their collecting efforts on obtaining small mammals for Joseph Grinnell and the Museum of Vertebrate Zoology by 1924, in the fall of that year the women took a fossil hunting expedition to Last Chance Canyon in California's Mojave Desert. After Kellogg quit her teaching job to become Alexander's full-time collecting partner in 1910, Annie and Louise usually traveled alone on their collecting trips. On the Last Chance expedition, however, they took along Annie's cousin, Mary Charlotte Alexander.

From the field, Mary Charlotte wrote exuberantly to her family regarding the beauty of the desert and the extraordinary skill, knowledge, and commitment that her older cousin Annie displayed as a collector:

> I can understand now why Annie loves the desert so much, and why it is particularly alluring to her with her rare scientific knowledge and insight. She has never yet made such a trip without finding some rare fossils that made it worthwhile. She says life will become prosaic later when everything is discovered! The uncovered, weathered strata here are something like an open book to her, as she knows the periods so well; she instantly gives the scientific name of any bone that we find, telling what animal it belonged to; and she recognizes the animal tracks and knows intimately all the birds we see. . . . The intense fascination of this work, I think lies in the fact that what we find has real scientific value, and as Annie says, "Throws light on a closed chapter of the world's history." She says that the place grows more and more interesting as we understand more of its significance.*

* Quoted in Barbara R. Stein, *On Her Own Terms: Annie Montague Alexander and the Rise of Science in the American West.* Berkeley: Univ. of California Press, 2001, p. 216–17.

the swiftness with which the two were able to put up high quality specimens was remarkable. Zoology professors at the University of California used to exhort their graduate students "to speed up their collecting efforts, to prepare at least ten specimens a day, because that was the rate that 'Miss Alexander and Miss Kellogg' maintained," notes Barbara Stein.[57]

THE IMPORTANCE OF THE WORK

Although Alexander was determined to build the Museum of Vertebrate Zoology into an internationally respected research center through her fieldwork as well as through her financial assistance, Annie had no interest in attaining personal recognition for her contributions to the museum or to science generally. Consequently, she refused to have her name included on the many articles and books that Grinnell and others at the museum published over the years using specimens that she had collected. Soon after establishing the MVZ, Annie also made it clear that she did not want any more new fossil or animal species named for her. Her wishes were not always followed by appreciative researchers, however, for by the time of Annie's death in 1950, 13 new fossil, animal, and plant species or subspecies had been named in her honor, 8 more than bore her name in 1909, when the MVZ opened its doors. Following Alexander's death, 4 additional species would also be named for her. As the historian Marcia Myers Bonta writes of Alexander, "It was obviously neither the desire for immortality through nomenclature that motivated Annie nor a thirst for fame." (Nomenclature is a system of names used in science or art.) For Annie Montague Alexander, notes Bonta, "the work was all that mattered."[58]

The rapidity with which Western lands were being irrigated and planted by farmers and fenced in by cattle ranchers and the resulting disturbance to the region's native fauna and flora lent a sense of urgency to Alexander's fieldwork during the 1920s and 1930s. In the regular reports that she sent to Grinnell whenever she was in the field, Alexander often noted instances of habitat perturbation and the disappearance of once common species from the West.

In 1931, for example, while on a collecting trip in Arizona, she wrote repeatedly to Grinnell regarding the alarming drop in the number of prairie dogs in that state. In Arizona, as in many other western states, the burrowing prairie dogs were widely considered as pests by ranchers and farmers. Consequently, they were being shot, trapped, and poisoned out of existence in many communities. By sheer persistence, Alexander and Kellogg finally located a small colony of a particularly rare species of the persecuted rodent, the black-tailed prairie dog, near the town of Willcox in eastern Arizona. Although the tiny colony was not even located on cultivated land, government agents had nonetheless scheduled it for extermination, Annie learned. Hoping to collect a few of the rare animals for the MVZ before it was too late, Alexander hastily set out a number of traps in the area and hired a local trapper to assist her. By the time the poisoning took place, she had succeeded in obtaining three specimens.

Grinnell was thrilled to receive Alexander's three black-tailed prairie dog specimens, calling them "prizes." He was, however, disgusted with the deliberate campaign to destroy prairie dog colonies in Willcox and throughout the West, even on land that was not being farmed or grazed: "I confess I cannot see why any kind of wild animal on *un*cultivated ground should be pursued to outright extinction," he wrote to Annie. Grinnell continued:

> I think such an act is a *crime*. I am all wrought up over the biological injustice of it! And the case which you have been witness to is only one of what promises to be a long series of willful extinctions.[59]

It may seem odd to us today that neither Grinnell nor Alexander discerned any contradiction in killing rare animals whose imminent extinction they obviously feared and regretted, but 75 years ago few people could have envisioned the current emphasis on preserving endangered species through captive breeding programs. Instead, Grinnell and Alexander thought in terms of merely preserving a *record* of vanishing species for posterity. Accordingly, soon after the founding of the Museum of Vertebrate Zoology, Grinnell wrote to Alexander:

> At this point I wish to emphasize what I believe will ultimately prove to be the greatest value of our museum. And this is that the student of the future will have access to the original record of faunal conditions in California and the West wherever we now work.[60]

A PASSION FOR THE DESERT

Increasingly during the 1920s and 1930s, Alexander preferred to collect in remote desert areas in California and throughout the American West, "that great, unreclaimable country . . . where there is nothing to tempt the enterprising spirit of man to conquer and subdue," according to Annie.[61] "I feel destined to become some day a recluse," she wrote to Martha during a long field trip in the deserts of Nevada. "The world is too much for me, too masterful. I fly from it to the lonely places that make no demand upon my [mental] strength."[62]

As Annie Alexander grew older, not only the tranquil solitude of the desert but its warm, dry climate increasingly suited her. So, too, did the desert's rugged beauty. Although some people might scorn the desert as barren and monotonous, Annie discovered much to admire in the harsh grandeur of its landscape. In her letters to friends and relatives, Annie extolled the unique charm of the windblown sand dunes where she and Louise often camped and collected, noting the striking symmetry of their ripple marks, how their fine grains shimmered in the moonlight, and the astonishing number of tiny rodent tracks that crisscrossed the huge expanses of white sand each dawn—proof that as desolate as the desert might appear, it was actually teeming with life.

On their long excursions into the arid regions of California, Nevada, Arizona, New Mexico, Colorado, Idaho, and Utah, Kellogg and Alexander collected a variety of small mammals for the MVZ including mice, voles, shrews, and gophers. One desert animal that the women hunted for food as well as for museum specimens was the kangaroo rat, which can measure up to 15 inches long from the tip of its nose to the end of its tufted tail. Like its namesake, the kangaroo rat has oversized back legs and feet that help it leap for long distances. The hind legs of just one of the large rodents, Alexander noted, provided her and Louise with more than enough meat for a meal and was every bit "as delicate and as good eating as chicken."[63]

THE RISKS AND THE REWARDS
OF AN "OUT-OF-DOOR LIFE"

Alexander and Kellogg faced numerous challenges working and camping out in the desert. On one collecting trip in Idaho, the temperature reached a brutal 136 degrees Fahrenheit. On another expedition to southwestern Utah, the women's thermometer registered 122 degrees in the shade. "We are sweltering," Annie wrote to her friend Edna Wemple McDonald. "It is one o'clock and two hours from now we must go out on the blazing hot hillside, pick up our traps and re-set them again."[64]

In many of the places Alexander and Kellogg visited, scorpions and venomous snakes posed a constant danger. Nonetheless, the women fearlessly slept out on the ground beneath the stars whenever the weather permitted. "Why not take risks now and then? It adds to the zest of life," Alexander once observed.[65] Matching her actions to her words, on one memorable occasion Annie snatched a rare ground squirrel she wanted for her museum right from the open jaws of a "rattlesnake that was about to swallow it whole," Kellogg reported admiringly in a letter to a friend.[66] (Kellogg was hardly timid around the venomous snakes herself. On a field trip to Nevada, Alexander noted, Louise, an avid fisherwoman, "noosed two large gopher snakes with her fish line and two rattlesnakes which were too helpless even to buzz their rattles when they were dangling in the air."[67])

Both Alexander and Kellogg were prepared to endure almost any discomfort or hazard in carrying out their work in the field, from driving rains to biting ants to angry rattlers. Even after turning 60 in 1927, Alexander was still ready and willing to climb steep mountains or traverse trackless deserts to obtain a specimen. "I consider the sixties a very appropriate period in one's life to do fieldwork," she assured the much younger Joseph Grinnell.[68] As if to prove her point, on a field trip to southwestern Utah in 1929 Alexander went out of her way to scale several of the loftiest and most rugged peaks in the Pine Valley range. "Every drop of blood in me . . . is for an active out-of-door life," the 37-year-old Alexander declared in 1905 as she prepared for her fourth fossil hunting expedition under the tutelage of John Merriam.[69] A quarter of a century later, Annie had not changed her mind regarding a nature-centered lifestyle: for her, she informed Joseph Grinnell, fieldwork was "an out-of-doors quest that will always have, I believe, a certain charm and excitement about it."[70]

Owing in large measure to Alexander and Kellogg's energetic and skillful fieldwork, within just two decades of its founding, the Museum of Vertebrate Zoology ranked third among all scientific institutions in the United States in the size of its mammal collections (after the American Museum of Natural History in New York City and the Biological Survey in Washington, D.C.). In its holdings of mammals indigenous to the western United States, the Museum of Vertebrate Zoology stood first in the entire world.

7

An Explorer
to the Last

A few months before the 30th anniversary of the founding of the MVZ, Annie Montague Alexander celebrated her 70th birthday. She did not intend to spend her "golden years" in a rocking chair, however. As she began her seventh decade of life, Alexander's passion for adventuring in the great outdoors was as strong as ever. Nor had her need to feel useful—to believe that she was making a significant contribution in the world—diminished with the passing of the years. Collecting specimens for her research museums "gave purpose to Alexander's life," writes Barbara Stein. "Without it, the freedom and pleasure that she experienced in the outdoors and found vital to her mental and physical well-being would have been little more than self-indulgence."[71]

STRANDED

During the winter of 1936–37, Alexander took one of the most memorable field trips of her long collecting career. In December, she and Kellogg set out for the arid regions of eastern California to collect small mammals for the Museum of Vertebrate Zoology. After spending a few weeks in the Mojave Desert, in late December they drove north toward the Saline Valley, a remote and rugged spot never before visited by collectors from the MVZ.

With a low point some 1,000 feet beneath the towering peaks that surround it on all sides, Saline Valley is one of the deepest enclosed basins in the world. After a slow and often harrowing drive down into the valley, Alexander and Kellogg made camp on the basin's sandy floor and diligently set out their traps. Almost immediately, the weather, which had been chilly but clear, took a turn for the worse. In the valley, it rained steadily; in the encircling mountains, the precipitation came in the form of snow. The inclement weather did not much bother Annie, but the poor trapping in the valley did. After a week of capturing discouragingly few animals, the women decided to pack up their automobile and head for a neighboring valley, where Alexander hoped their collecting efforts would prove more productive. To the pair's dismay, however, they soon discovered that the roads leading out of Saline Valley were blocked by deep, drifting snow.

In search of assistance, Alexander and Kellogg hiked a few miles up the canyon to a mining camp that they had noticed a week earlier on their way into Saline. The miners were stranded as well, however: even their big trucks could not break through the heavy snow that clogged the valley's roads. Although Alexander politely declined the miners' offer to stay in a vacant shack near their camp until help could arrive, she did borrow a few cans of food from the men.

Back at their campsite on the valley floor, Alexander and Kellogg spent much of their waking hours gathering and chopping firewood. Since there was no snow down in the valley, they hiked a mile and a half up and down the canyon each day to fill their pails with snow for drinking water. As the days and weeks crawled by, the women's food supply dwindled to a few cans of beans and some cornmeal.

Meanwhile, back in Berkeley, Joseph Grinnell was becoming increasingly worried. Annie always communicated regularly with him when she was in the field, yet an entire month had passed since her last letter. Finally, Grinnell decided to send two young museum employees, Ward Russell and Bill Richardson, to the Saline Valley, where he knew Alexander and Kellogg had been headed as of late December. He also mailed a letter to Annie in care of the post office at Big Pine, the closest town to the remote valley. Keenly aware of Alexander's proud and independent spirit, Grinnell was determined not to offend her, as his carefully worded missive reveals:

> I have decided to launch a "field trip" . . . to get first-hand information that will reassure friends of you [*sic*] and Miss Kellogg, who are, I am convinced, truly suffering from *worry*. . . . I know . . . that you and Miss Kellogg are thoroly [*sic*] well qualified field people—[able] to care

for yourselves under any sort of conditions imposed by nature. But worry (on the part of others) is, more or less, a human attribute. [72]

When Richardson and Russell arrived in Big Pine and heard that the roads in and out of the valley were completely blocked, they hired Norman Clyde, a winter explorer and skilled cross-country skier, to search for Alexander and Kellogg. It took Clyde two days to ski from Big Pine to the mining camp where the women had sought assistance. He was amazed to discover that the women were not staying with the miners but instead had chosen to remain by themselves on the valley floor.

The next morning, Clyde made his way down to Alexander and Kellogg's campsite. A grateful and clearly relieved Alexander promptly sent him back to Richardson and Russell with a check for $100 to be used for hiring a caterpillar tractor to get her automobile, and her and Kellogg, out of the valley. Four days later, the men returned with the tractor and the women's month-long ordeal was finally over.

Alexander and Kellogg's experience in Saline Valley did not deter the intrepid partners from embarking on another winter camping and collecting expedition the following year in the Mojave Desert. This field trip in search of pocket gophers for Joseph Grinnell's current research on the geographical distribution of those burrowing mammals proved highly successful. (The pocket gopher's unusual name refers to the roomy pouches on the outside of its cheeks, which it uses for transporting nesting material and food.) Before Annie and Louise's expedition, pocket gophers were believed to be rare in the Mojave. After capturing nearly 100 specimens of the rodents from 23 different localities, however, the women were able to demonstrate that pocket gophers were widely distributed throughout the Mojave. The following winter, the pair returned to the Mojave Desert one last time, gathering another 128 specimens of pocket gophers for the MVZ's collections.

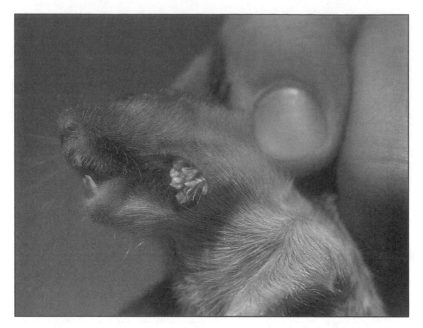

At the age of 70, Alexander was still exploring, and in 1936 she embarked on a trip to eastern California to study small mammals. Her search for pocket gophers was extremely successful, and she and her companions disproved the assumption that these animals were rare in the Mojave. Pocket gophers, like the one seen here storing flower petals in its cheek, are named for the roomy pouches on their cheeks that store food and nesting material.

A NEW DIRECTION

In May 1939, Alexander received a devastating blow when Joseph Grinnell died of a heart attack at the age of 62. It was hard for Annie to conceive that "the man who has had such an influence on my life" was actually gone.[73] "We have been so closely united in our ambition to make the Museum a center for the study of vertebrate zoology with a reputation for high quality output that his sudden death leaves me stranded in a way," a stunned Alexander confided to Martha Beckwith.[74] To Joseph's wife, Hilda, Annie wrote glowingly of her three-decade-long relationship with the man whom she had personally chosen to direct the MVZ:

> Throughout the years he never seemed to lose sight of the
> fact that I was his backer in this splendid and inspiring
> enterprise, was ever solicitous to keep me in touch with
> what was transpiring at the Museum, to shield me from
> worry and that I should share in all the triumphs that
> came our way. [75]

During his long tenure as director, Grinnell not only
consulted Alexander regarding all MVZ expenditures, staff
changes, and new fieldwork and research plans, he also
enthusiastically encouraged and advised her in her own
collecting endeavors for the museum. Although Alexander
respected Alden Miller, Grinnell's replacement at the MVZ,
she never developed the kind of close professional and
personal relationship with Alden that she had enjoyed with
Joseph, and after 1939, her involvement with the museum
decreased markedly.

Soon after Grinnell's death, Alexander decided to redirect
her collecting efforts from zoological to botanical specimens.
She found much to relish in her new line of fieldwork, as she
explained to Hilda Grinnell in 1940, "I like the mechanical
work of drying specimens, the walks through the woods, the
sunshine that strikes through the pines in the early mornings
and I dread going back to the city." [76]

The end of the Grinnell era at the MVZ coincided with
another change in direction for Annie Alexander. After
Grinnell's death, Alexander showed a new interest in making
fieldwork opportunities available to female graduate students
and employees at the University of California. Although
Grinnell had made no secret of his profound respect for
Alexander and Kellogg's abilities in the field, he clearly considered
them as the exceptions to the rule as far as female collectors
were concerned. Most women, Grinnell firmly believed, were
not suited to the rigors and discomforts of life in the field,
and throughout his 31-year tenure at the MVZ, he refused to

allow women graduate students or employees to take part in museum-sponsored field expeditions.

We have no way of knowing why Alexander chose to tolerate Grinnell's exclusionary policies at the MVZ regarding women and museum-sponsored fieldwork. Reserved by nature, Annie was reticent about expressing her personal feelings and attitudes regarding many controversial subjects, including women's rights, in her correspondence and even in her diaries. Between 1941 and 1942, however, she went a long way toward making up for her earlier disregard for the barriers facing females in her museum by generously funding three field trips to different locales in California for women graduate students at the MVZ.

Five years later, in 1947, Alexander decided to sponsor and participate in an ambitious field trip for a female botanist at the University of California named Annetta Carter. This trip to the Mexican state of Baja, California, would prove to be Alexander's last great collecting adventure.

BAJA CALIFORNIA AND ANNETTA CARTER

Throughout most of the twentieth century, opportunities for female scientists in the United States remained depressingly meager. Most women scientists were employed as teachers at women's colleges; few proved able to obtain research, teaching, or administrative positions at coed colleges or universities. Annetta Carter, who held a master's degree in botany from the University of California, had managed to secure an important position at Berkeley's University herbarium, where she was responsible for the facility's day-to-day operations. Nonetheless, as of 1947, the 40-year-old Carter had never been offered the opportunity to participate in university-sponsored fieldwork, an oversight that Annetta was convinced had everything to do with her gender. Thus, when Alexander invited Carter to accompany her and Kellogg on a three-month-long botanical collecting trip to the Baja peninsula, Annetta jumped at the chance.

In 1947, Baja California was one of the most rugged and sparsely populated regions in North America, exactly the kind of place that appealed to the adventurous Alexander, even at the age of 79. Seven-hundred-sixty-miles (760) long, the Baja peninsula is bounded by the Gulf of California (also known as the Sea of Cortez) to the east and the Pacific Ocean to the west. Although most of the land consists of deserts or rugged mountain ranges, Baja, California, boasts an abundant and fascinating flora. Many of the plants that flourish in its vast deserts grow nowhere else in the world.

On November 3, 1947, Alexander, Kellogg, and Carter drove across the California border into Mexico at Tijuana in the sturdy, four-wheel drive Dodge "power wagon" that Alexander had specially purchased to traverse the peninsula's rough dirt roads. Over the next six weeks, the women slowly made their way to the southern tip of the peninsula at Cabo San Lucas, stopping often to gather interesting plants, shoot photographs, or take a refreshing dip in the ocean. Every evening "whenever darkness was about to overtake us," Carter later wrote, they scouted out a place to camp near the roadside "where there weren't too many cacti or rocks."[77]

On their journey back north through the peninsula, the women took a week-long backpacking trip into the Sierra de la Laguna mountain range. One of the highlights of the excursion for Annie was climbing to the summit of Cerro Picacho de la Laguna, which at approximately 7,000 feet is the tallest peak in the Sierra de la Laguna range. On December 29, Annie's 80th birthday, the hikers came down from the mountains and resumed their long drive northward.

In late January, after almost three months in the field, the women returned home to California. They carried with them more than 4,600 plant specimens, including a number of never-before-described species. The trip would have an enormous impact on Annetta Carter's career as a botanist. Inspired by her 1947 expedition with Annie Alexander, Carter returned to Baja, California, almost every year thereafter to collect new plant specimens. Eventually, Carter would become one of the world's leading experts on the unique flora of that region.

"I CAN'T GO YET"

During the two years following the Baja, California, expedition, Annie took a series of shorter field trips in California in search of botanical specimens for the University herbarium, including a camping trip to the rugged Trinity Mountains during the summer of 1948. Never mind that she was now in her 80s. "It is better to wear out than to rust out," Alexander liked to say.[78] In the summer of 1948, Alexander also established two permanent scholarships for graduate students in the

FOSSIL, MAMMAL, AND PLANT SPECIES NAMED FOR ANNIE MONTAGUE ALEXANDER

Shastasaurus alexandrae: fossil (1902)

Thalattosaurus alexandrae: fossil (1904)

Acrodus alexandrae: fossil (1906)

Lagopus alexandrae: bird (1909)

Ilingoceros alexandrae: fossil (1909)

Aplodontia alexandrae: fossil (1910)

Ursus alexandrae: mammal (1914)

Alticamelus alexandrae: fossil (1923)

Sitta carolinensis alexandrae: bird (1926)

Thomomys alexandrae: mammal (1933)

Hydrotherosaurus alexandrae: fossil (1943)

Lupinus alexandrae: plant (1944)

Swallenia alexandrae: plant (1950)

Bouvardia alexandrae: plant (1955)

Scaphiopus alexanderi: fossil (1956)

Mojavemys alexandrae: fossil (1972)

Eriogonum ochrocephalum: plant (1985)

Museum of Vertebrate Zoology and the University of California Museum of Paleontology.

In the spring of 1949, while on a botanical collecting trip in the Eureka Valley in eastern California, Alexander made an extraordinary find. Scouring the lower slopes of a large sand dune, she spotted an unfamiliar-looking coarse grass. When the botanists at the University herbarium could not identify the unusual specimen, they sent the plant on to the Smithsonian in Washington, D.C. Smithsonian researchers declared the grass to be an extremely rare find, a brand new species that they named *Swallenia alexandrae* in honor of Alexander.

On November 6, 1949, Alexander's long and productive career as a field biologist finally ended when she suffered a massive stroke. According to one account, Alexander's last words before lapsing into a coma a few days later were, "I can't go yet, I'm not finished."[79] Annie Montague Alexander died on September 10, 1950, exactly 46 years to the day after her beloved father's death in Africa. A grief-stricken Louise Kellogg, Annie's almost constant companion for four decades, arranged for Alexander's remains to be sent back to her childhood home of Maui for burial.

More than 50 years later, Annie Montague Alexander's legacy lives on. The two museums that Alexander founded and generously endowed at Berkeley and whose collections she did so much to build through her own energetic fieldwork, remain vital centers of scientific research and learning. The Museum of Vertebrate Zoology currently houses some 700,000 skeletons, study skins, and a collection of mammal specimens that is virtually without equal. The University of California's Museum of Paleontology is also thriving; its vast and continually expanding collections of vertebrate, invertebrate, and plant fossils are ranked among the best in the world. These two internationally renowned museums provide ample testimony that in her quest to do something useful with her life and make a lasting contribution, Annie Montague Alexander was remarkably successful.

Chronology

1867   Born on December 29 in Honolulu, Hawaii

1870   Father, Samuel Alexander starts successful sugar plantation on Maui

1883   Moves to Oakland, California, with family

1887–9   Attends Lasell Seminary for Young Women in Auburndale, Massachusetts

1899   Ten-week camping trip to Northern California and Southern Oregon

TIMELINE

1867
Born in Honolulu, Hawaii, on December 29

1908
Third zoological collecting expedition to Alaska; first with longtime partner Louise Kellogg

Establishes Museum of Vertebrate Zoology at University of California at Berkeley

1860   **1880**   **1890**   **1900**

1901
Participates in her first paleontological field trip to Fossil Lake, Oregon

1904
Hunting safari in British East Africa with father Samuel, who dies on the trip

1900 Begins auditing courses in paleontology with Professor John C. Merriam at University of California at Berkeley

1901 Finances and takes part in first fossil-collecting trip to Fossil Lake, Oregon

1904 Samuel Alexander dies while on safari with Annie in British East Africa

1906 First collecting and hunting expedition to Alaska

1921
Establishes University of California Museum of Paleontology as separate unit at the Berkeley campus

1950
Dies on September 10 at age 82

1920   1940   1950

1947
Celebrates 80th birthday in the field during a three-month trip to Baja California to collect plant specimens

Chronology

1908 Third collecting trip to Alaska and first expedition with Louise Kellogg

1908 Donates funds for a natural history museum at the University of California

1909 Museum of Vertebrate Zoology (MVZ) officially opens its doors with Joseph Grinnell as director

1911 Starts farm on Grizzly Island with Louise Kellogg

1919 Establishes an endowment for the MVZ

1921 Funds University of California Museum of Paleontology (UCMP) as independent unit on Berkeley campus

1934 Establishes endowment for the UCMP

1936–7 Snowbound for a month in California's remote Saline Valley

1939 Joseph Grinnell, director of the MVZ for more than three decades, dies

1947 Undertakes three-month long collecting trip to Baja California with Kellogg and botanist Annetta Carter; celebrates 80th birthday in the field

1950 Dies on September 10 at age 82

Notes

Chapter One

1. Quoted in Barbara R. Stein, *On Her Own Terms: Annie Montague Alexander and the Rise of Science in the American West* (Berkeley: Univ. of California Press, 2001), 190.

Chapter Two

2. Ibid., 5.

3. Ibid., 15.

Chapter Three

4. Ibid., 10.

5. Ibid., 10.

6. Ibid., 28.

7. Quoted in Barbara Miller Solomon, *In the Company of Educated Women: A History of Women and Higher Education in America* (New Haven: Yale Univ. Press, 1985), 56.

8. Quoted in Donald J. Winslow, *Lasell: A History of the First Junior College for Women* (Boston: Nimrod Press, 1987), 56.

9. Quoted in Margaret W. Rossiter, *Women Scientists in America: Struggles and Strategies to 1940* (Baltimore: Johns Hopkins Univ. Press, 1982), xvi.

10. Winslow, *Lasell,* 22.

11. Quoted in Stein, *On Her Own Terms,* 20.

12. Ibid., 20.

13. Quoted in Donna R. Braden, *Leisure and Entertainment in America* (Dearborn, MI: Henry Ford Museum, 1988), 317–18.

14. Quoted in Gretel Ehrlich, *John Muir: Nature's Visionary* (Washington, D.C.: National Geographic, 2000), 173.

Chapter Four

15. Quoted in Marcia Myers Bonta, *Women in the Field: America's Pioneering Women Naturalists.* (College Station, TX: Texas A and M Univ. Press, 1991), 50.

16. Quoted in Stein, *On Her Own Terms,* 110–11.

17. Ibid., 51.

18. Ibid., 27.

19. Ibid., 28.

20. Ibid., 29.

21. Quoted in Bonta, *Women in the Field.,* 50.

22. Ibid., 51.

23. Ibid., 50.

24. Quoted in Stein, *On Her Own Terms,* 35.

25. Quoted in Brian Herne, *White Hunters: The Golden Age of the African Safaris* (New York: Henry Holt, 1999), 45.

26. Quoted in Stein, *On Her Own Terms,* 42–43.

27. Ibid., 45.

28. Ibid., 43.

29. Ibid., 39.

30. Ibid., 40.

31. Ibid., 43.

32. Ibid., 43–44.

33. Ibid., 45

34. Ibid., 47.

Chapter Five

35. Ibid., 188.

36. Quoted in "Annie Montague Alexander: Benefactress of UCMP", *http://www.ucmp.berkeley. edu/history/alexander.html*

Notes

37. Ibid.

38. Quoted in Bonta, *Women in the Field*, 52.

39. Quoted in Stein, *On Her Own Terms*, 51.

40. Quoted in "Saurian Expedition of 1905", *http://www.ucmp.berkeley. edu/archives/saurian.html*

41. Quoted in Milbry Polk and Mary Tiegreen, *Women of Discovery: A Celebration of Intrepid Women Who Explored the World* (New York: Clarkson Potter), 2001, 91.

42. Quoted in Stein, *On Her Own Terms*, 48.

43. Quoted in Bonta, *Women in the Field*, 53.

44. Quoted in Stein, *On Her Own Terms*, 99.

45. Quoted in Bonta, *Women in the Field*, 54.

46. Quoted in Stein, *On Her Own Terms*, 102.

47. Ibid., 106.

48. Quoted in Bonta, *Women in the Field*, 53.

49. Quoted in Stein, *On Her Own Terms*, 55.

50. Ibid., 75.

51. Quoted in "MVZ History", *http://www.mip.berkeley.edu/ mvz/history*

52. Quoted in Stein, *On Her Own Terms*, 80.

Chapter Six
53. Ibid., 122.

54. Ibid., 182.

55. Ibid., 166.

56. Quoted in *http://www.ucmp.berkeley. edu/history*

57. Stein, *On Her Own Terms*, 149.

58. Bonta, *Women in the Field*, 57.

59. Quoted in Stein, *On HerOwn Terms*, 239.

60. Ibid., 150.

61. Quoted in Bonta, *Women in the Field*, 56.

62. Quoted in Stein, *On HerOwn Terms*, 222.

63. Ibid., 227.

64. Ibid., 234.

65. Quoted in Bonta, *Women in the Field*, 51

66. Quoted in Stein, *On Her Own Terms*, 237.

67. Quoted in Bonta, *Women in the Field*, 57.

68. Ibid., 58.

69. Quoted in Stein, *On Her Own Terms*, 50.

70. Quoted in Bonta, *Women in the Field*, 58.

Chapter Seven
71. Quoted in Stein, *On Her Own Terms*, 148.

72. Ibid., 249.

73. Quoted in Bonta, *Women in the Field*, 58.

74. Quoted in Stein, *On Her Own Terms*, 253.

75. Ibid., 254.

76. Quoted in Bonta, *Women in the Field*, 59.

77. Ibid., 60.

78. Quoted in Stein, *On Her Own Terms*, 226.

79. Ibid., 358.

Books

Abir-am, Pnina G., and Dorinda Outram, eds. *Uneasy Careers and Intimate Lives: Women in Science, 1789–1979.* New Brunswick, N.J.: Rutgers University Press, 1987.

Bisignani, J.D. *Maui Handbook.* Chico, Calif.: Moon Publications, 1999.

Bonta, Marcia Myers. *Women in the Field: America's Pioneering Women Naturalists.* College Station, Texas: Texas A and M University Press, 1991.

Braden, Donna R. *Leisure and Entertainment in America.* Dearborn, Mich.: Henry Ford Museum, 1988.

Ehrlich, Gretel. *John Muir: Nature's Visionary.* Washington, D.C.: National Geographic, 2000.

Grinnell, Hilda W. *Annie Montague Alexander.* Berkeley: Grinnell Naturalists Society, 1958.

Herne, Brian. *White Hunters: The Golden Age of the African Safaris.* New York: Henry Holt, 1999.

Milner, Clyde A., Carol A. O'Connor, and Martha A. Sandweiss, eds. *The Oxford History of the American West.* New York: Oxford University Press, 1994.

Polk, Milbry and Mary Tiegreen, *Women of Discovery: A Celebration of Intrepid Women Who Explored the World.* New York: Clarkson Potter, 2001.

Rossiter, Margaret W. *Women Scientists in America: Before Affirmative Action.* Baltimore: Johns Hopkins University Press, 1995.

———, *Women Scientists in America: Struggles and Strategies to 1940.* Baltimore: Johns Hopkins University Press, 1982.

Solomon, Barbara Miller. *In the Company of Educated Women: A History of Women and Higher Education in America.* New Haven: Yale University Press, 1985.

Stein, Barbara R. *On Her Own Terms: Annie Montague Alexander and the Rise of Science in the American West.* Berkeley: University of California Press, 2001.

Winslow, Donald J. *Lasell: A History of the First Junior College for Women.* Boston: Nimrod Press, 1987.

Bibliography

Websites
Hawaiian Commercial and Sugar Company: History
http://www.hcsugar.com/history.html

Lasell College: History
http://www.lassel.edu/about/history

Museum of Vertebrate Zoology: History: Annie Montague Alexander
http://www.mip.berkeley.edu/mvz/history

Natural Hawaii
http://www.naturalhawaii.com

Saurian Expedition of 1905
http://www.ucmp.berkeley.edu/archives/saurian.html

Sanders, Robert. "A Birthday for a Library of Bones"
http://www.berkeley.edu/news/berkeleyan/1996/1009/bones.htm

University of California Museum of Paleontology: History: Annie Alexander
http://www.ucmp.berkeley.edu/history/alexander.html

Bonta, Marcia Myers. *Women in the Field: America's Pioneering Women Naturalists.* College Station, Texas: Texas A and M University Press, 1991.

Polk, Milbry, and Mary Tiegreen. *Women of Discovery: A Celebration of Intrepid Women Who Explored the World.* New York: Clarkson Potter, 2001.

Stein, Barbara R. *On Her Own Terms: Annie Montague Alexander and the Rise of Science in the American West.* Berkeley: University of California Press, 2001.

Index

Index

and Alexander's trip to
Crater Lake, 28
and Museum of Vertebrate
Zoology, 3
botany, 3.
See also University herbarium
British East Africa. *See* East
Africa

C & H (Californian and
Hawaiian) sugar, 20
California
Alexander collecting botani-
cal specimens in Baja in,
80–83
Alexander collecting botani-
cal specimens in Eureka
Valley in, 83
Alexander collecting speci-
mens for Museum of
Vertebrate Zoology in, 3,
66, 71
Alexander organizing and
funding fossil hunting
expeditions in Shasta
County in, 35–36
Alexander spending teenage
years in Oakland in, 2, 17,
19–21
Alexander spending winters
in, 65
Alexander stranded in Saline
Valley in, 75–77
Alexander's camping trip in
Northern part of, 26–29
Alexander's father gold min-
ing in, 10
Alexander's father's sugar-
cane business in, 19–20
Alexander's Grizzly Island
farm in, 63–65

and demand for Hawaiian
sugar, 9–10, 13, 19–20
and gold rush, 10.
See also University of
California at Berkeley
camping, and Alexander
and collecting specimens for
Museum of Vertebrate
Zoology, 66–67, 69–73,
75–77
and Fossil Lake expedition,
33–34
and trip to Northern
California and Southern
Oregon, 26–29.
See also fossil hunting
expeditions, Alexander
organizing and funding
Carter, Annetta, 80–83
Cascade Mountain range,
Alexander seeing on camp-
ing trip, 28–29
cattle, and Alexander's Grizzly
Island farm, 64–65
Cerro Picacho de la Laguna,
Alexander climbing, 81
Chichagof Island, and
Alexander's expedition to
Alaska, 50, 51
China, Alexander traveling to
with father, 26
Clarke, Edward, 21
Clyde, Norman, 77
Crater Lake, Alexander's
camping expedition to,
26–29

dark continent. *See* East Africa
Darwin, Charles, 55
desert, Alexander collecting
specimens in, 71–72, 77

94

Index

Index

Index

Picture Credits

Contributors

Louise Chipley Slavicek received her master's degree in history from the University of Connecticut. She has written many articles on historical topics for young people's magazines and is the author of eight other books for young people, including *Women of the Revolutionary War, Israel, Abraham Lincoln,* and *Jimmy Carter.* She lives in Ohio with her husband Jim, a research biologist, and their two children, Krista and Nathan.

Series consulting editor **Milbry Polk** graduated from Harvard in 1976. An explorer all her life, she has ridden horseback through Pakistan's Northwest Territories, traveled with Bedouin tribesmen in Jordan and Egypt, surveyed Arthurian sites in Wales, and trained for the first Chinese-American canoe expedition. In 1979, supported by the National Geographic Society, Polk led a camel expedition retracing the route of Alexander the Great across Egypt.

Her work as a photojournalist has appeared in numerous magazines, including Time, Fortune, Cosmopolitan and Quest. Currently she is a contributing editor to the *Explorers Journal.* Polk is a Fellow of the Royal Geographic Society and a Fellow of the Explorers Club. She is the also the author of two award-winning books, *Egyptian Mummies* (Dutton Penguin, 1997) and *Women of Discovery* (Clarkson Potter, 2001).

Milbry Polk serves as an advisor to the George Polk Awards for Journalistic Excellence, is on the Council of the New York Hall of Science, serves on the Board of Governors of the National Arts Club, the Children's Shakespeare Theater Board and is the director of Wings World Quest. She lives in Palisades, New York, with her husband and her three daughters. She and her daughters row on the Hudson River.